Roger Cox has been writing ab
2005 and has contributed a wee
majoring on surfing and snows]
arts editor since 2013. In 202
at the British Journalism Awai
Sessions – a series of video pe
around Scotland and introduced by *Scotsman* critics. His royal-
ties from this book are being donated to the marine conservation
organisation Surfers Against Sewage (www.sas.org.uk).

The View from the Shoulder

A Portrait of Scottish Surfing

Roger Cox

First published in 2025 by
Arena Sport, an imprint of
Birlinn Limited
West Newington House
10 Newington Road
Edinburgh
EH9 1QS
www.arenasportbooks.co.uk

ISBN 978 1 913759 24 7

British Library Cataloguing-in-Publication Data
A catalogue record for this book is available from the British Library

Typeset by Initial Typesetting Services, Edinburgh

Papers used by Birlinn are from well-managed forests
and other responsible sources

Printed and bound by Page Bros Group Ltd, Norwich

Front cover: Craig McLachlan competing at the 2023 Scottish National Surfing
Championships at Brims Ness (Malcolm Anderson)
Back cover: Mark Boyd at Thurso East (Malcolm Anderson)

Contents

'The ultimate thing for most of us would be to have an endless summer: the warm water and waves, without the summer crowds of California.'

Bruce Brown, *The Endless Summer*, 1966

'In 1968 I found a company that sold neoprene rubber with drawings of how to cut out a wetsuit. It was more or less a diving wetsuit though, with a big flap at the front with buttons. . . It was extremely uncomfortable, but it was warmer than not having a wetsuit.'

Bill Batten, Scottish surfing pioneer,
Shackleton's Bar, Edinburgh, 2018

Introduction

A BIG part of the allure of Western surf culture, as crystallised in the music of the Beach Boys and the films of Bruce Brown, is its seductive promise of a never-ending summer. In marketing terms, it's genius. Want to sell something to the millions of people living in cold, dark, northern cities? Then pitch them sunshine! Pitch them warmth! Pitch them palm trees! Surfing, a sport which originated and evolved in the world's balmier latitudes, promises all of that, plus a side-order of adrenaline. No wonder they put it on a T-shirt.

But even as the dream was in the process of being sold, it was also in the process of being lost. In the middle of the 20th century, as surfing enjoyed an explosion of popularity along the sun-kissed, wave-rich coastlines of California and Australia, the best spots started to become crowded. Bruce Brown's iconic 1966 film *The Endless Summer* may start out as a celebration of California surf culture, but ultimately it's about trying to escape from it – first to Senegal, Ghana and Nigeria, then to Australia, New Zealand, Tahiti and Hawaii. The iconic climax of the film arrives when Brown and his two travelling surf stars, Mike Hynson and Robert August, discover perfect *empty* waves breaking at Cape St Francis in South Africa. 'Nothing at all there,' as Brown later put it, 'just perfect waves.'

The seek-and-ye-shall-find philosophy of *The Endless Summer* inspired a whole generation of surf explorers to go looking for their own untouched nirvana, and new warm water surf paradises were soon located, from Costa Rica and Mexico to Indonesia and Sri Lanka. Inevitably, however, these locations soon started to attract crowds of their own, and so the gaze of the surf-seekers began to shift elsewhere. Improvements in wetsuit technology (double-lined neoprene in the 1970s, blind-stitched seams in the 1980s) meant surfers could spend more time immersed in cold water, and so the search for uncrowded waves was extended to chillier parts of the globe. Iceland, Norway, Newfoundland and Alaska have all been on the surfing map for years, as have the southernmost reaches of Chile and Argentina.

Although Scotland got its first mention in Surfer magazine, the California-based Bible of the sport, back in the 1960s, it was as part of this second, cold-water wave of surf exploration that it truly became part of the global surfing consciousness. Surfing's great free-thinker Derek Hynd played a major role in raising the profile of the sport here when he held an experimental surf contest on the Isle of Lewis in 1991, featuring some of the top pros of the day including three-time world champion Tom Curren, and any lingering doubts about whether Scotland might be a legitimate surfing destination were blown clean out of the water in 1996, when Surfer ran an extensive travel story on Scotland's north coast, showing another posse of pros, including Curren's little brother, Joe, enjoying heavenly conditions on the north coast.

In spite of all this, however, when I first started writing about surfing in Scotland two decades ago plenty of people still seemed to think it was the punchline to a bad joke. One spring afternoon in the mid-noughties, driving along the coast of Sutherland after an idyllic solo surf, I remember turning on Radio Scotland and listening to a couple of presenters having a good chuckle about the fact that American pro surfer Rusty Long was hunting for big waves on the Isle of Lewis. Had he somehow become lost on his way to somewhere warmer, they wondered? Not long afterwards, while covering one of the first professional surf contests ever to be held in Scotland, with more than £35,000 of prize money up for grabs, I witnessed a Scottish TV presenter concluding a piece to camera by stripping down to his boxers and running into the sea in order to confirm that, yes, the water in the Pentland Firth is indeed chilly in April. Hard to imagine him being required to confirm the air temperature at an international rugby match at Murrayfield in the same way.

Just for the avoidance of doubt then: yes, the water off the coast of Scotland is indeed cold, relatively speaking, but wetsuits work, and have been doing so for decades. There's nothing weird about wanting to go surfing here. What *is* weird is that, with more than 11,000 miles of coastline (if you're counting all the islands), much of it exposed to the second largest ocean on earth, it's taken so long for the idea of surfing in Scotland to gain mainstream acceptance.

To be fair to the naysayers, in the early years of the new millennium surfing was even more of a minority sport in Scotland than it is now, and if anything, it appeared to be going backwards. Scottish surfing's governing body, the Scottish Surfing Federation (SSF), founded in the early 1970s, had only just emerged from a five-year hiatus, which had meant no national competitions to bring Scotland's scattered surfing tribes together between 2000 and 2004.

Fast-forward two decades to the present day, however, and the picture is very different. Spots that would have been all-but empty on a good swell in 2005 are now teeming with enthusiastic wave-riders. Scotland has its first pro surfer, Tiree's Ben Larg, who is paid to travel the world riding giant waves by multinational action sports company Red Bull. Another surfer, Andy Hadden, has just opened Europe's largest artificial wave pool, the Lost Shore surf resort, in a former quarry at Ratho near Edinburgh. With a price tag of £60million, it's the most ambitious sports infrastructure project completed in Scotland since the Commonwealth Arena and Sir Chris Hoy Velodrome in Glasgow in 2012. Thanks to a reinvigorated SSF, Scotland now has a lively contest scene, and our top surfers have shown they can hold their own against the best in the world at international competitions like Eurosurf and the World Surfing Games.

The idea of what a surfer looks like has also changed: there are far more women in the water now than there were 20 years ago, not to mention more kids and more people of retirement age and beyond. And Scotland's surfing population hasn't just grown, it's also grown up. These days, surfers are GPs and hospital consultants, teachers and university professors. This isn't just a sport practised by a few thrill-seeking twenty-somethings any more, if it ever was – it's woven into almost every aspect of Scottish life. Even the First Minister John Swinney is a surfer. Cling to the lazy stereotypes if you like, but these days surfers are literally running the country.

*

I first joined *The Scotsman* newspaper as a junior reporter in the summer of 2000, and officially I've worked on the arts desk ever since. Unofficially, though, I've also been writing about surfing for the paper since 2005, first on an ad-hoc basis for the features pages and then, from 2009 onwards, in a weekly outdoors column in Saturday magazine. In my two decades of sporadic surf scribbling the Scottish scene has changed out of all recognition, but this period is only the tail-end of a much longer story. Over the years, I've been lucky enough to interview several of the early pioneers of Scottish surfing, from Andy Bennetts, Ian Wishart and Bill Batten, who were among the first wave-riders on the east coast, to Shetlander Vince Attfield, who, on a walk home from the pub with a group of friends one night in the early 1990s, decided that it was about time somebody tried surfing in Scotland's most northerly archipelago, and that it might as well be them. These interviews form the basis of the first chapter of this book, which sketches out Scotland's early surfing history.

The second chapter deals with surf contests, from lighthearted affairs like the retro board contests held by the folks at Coast to Coast Surf School at Belhaven Bay near Dunbar to serious professional events with life-changing amounts of prize money at stake. It also charts the attempts of the Scottish Surfing Federation to gain recognition for Scotland as an independent surfing nation – a goal they finally achieved in 2014 – and the overseas exploits of the national team in the years that followed. There are, of course, plenty of people within the surfing community both here and elsewhere who don't see the point of surf contests. Surely, they argue, surfing is a spiritual activity that doesn't require timed heats, trophies and somebody on the beach shouting out scores after every wave. Those who don't choose to surf competitively – the vast majority – are known as freesurfers, and Chapter Three focuses on non-contest surfing.

Since Scotland first started to embrace surfing in the 1960s, it has developed its own distinctive surf culture, with its own art, films and literature. Chapter Four includes interviews with artists like Ross Ryan and Laura Maynard, who have committed

Scotland's waves and its surfers to canvas, and it also takes in some of the films, music, books and magazines the scene has produced over the last 20 years.

Finally, Chapter Five looks at the entrepreneurs of Scottish surfing as well as its innovators and its activists – the people looking for ways to move the sport forward, and those who seek to protect the marine environment on which its future depends. At the beginning of the 21st century, the Scottish surf industry consisted of little more than a handful of surf shops and surf schools dotted around the country. Since then, however, it has grown to incorporate surfboard shapers like Jason Burnett and homegrown surf brands like Staunch. And then, of course, in the autumn of 2024, the Lost Shore surf resort opened to the public, serving up 1,000 perfectly sculpted waves an hour using state-of-the-art Wavegarden technology, completely transforming Scotland's surfing ecosystem. This final chapter concludes with a series of interviews with some of the people who brought the Lost Shore project to fruition, and a report on the day it opened to the public.

*

One of the interviews in the Lost Shore series is with the wave pool's founder Andy Hadden, and his final quote is significant: 'The better you get [at surfing], the adventure only gets bigger, because you can start looking around the coast and things really open up. That's one of the things I'm most excited about seeing, people starting out on their own surfing journeys.' It's hard to say exactly what kind of long-term impact Lost Shore will have, but two things seem almost certain: first, the total number of surfers in Scotland is going to increase dramatically, and second, the standard of surfing is going to go through the roof. Assuming both these things happen, it seems likely that

Scotland's 'known' surf spots, some of which are already crowded, will become even more so as those who have developed their skills in the wave pool decide to head to the coast. If the last few decades of surfing history have taught us anything, however, it's that crowding only leads to more exploration, and happily the surfing potential of Scotland's great, long, rambling, drawn-by-a-drunken-monkey coastline is only just beginning to be realised.

In the autumn of 2024 I spoke to Ben Larg about a recent trip to Ireland, where he had ridden giant waves at Mullaghmore. I asked him if there were any other places out there in the wider surfing world that he was keen to explore, wondering if he might express an interest in Hawaii, still considered by many to be the ultimate proving ground for big wave surfers, or if he might have some remote South Pacific atoll in his sights. 'I'm keen to adventure round Scotland,' he said. 'I think some of the islands – maybe Lewis or Orkney – could be a good shout. So yeah, I'm gonna start having a scope, maybe try and find some new big waves.' What will surfing in Scotland look like 20 years from now? Impossible to say. It does seem likely, though, that we might end up with a few more pins in the map, courtesy of the next generation of Scottish surf pioneers.

Edinburgh, May 2025

A note on the text

All the stories in the following pages first appeared in either *The Scotsman* or *The Scotsman Magazine*. The introductions have been freshly written to provide context and, where necessary, to explain what happened next. The dates refer to the date of initial publication. Just as this book was going to press, the Scottish Surfing Federation (SSF) changed its name to Scottish Surfing.

A note on the title

One of the most commonly regurgitated cliches about surfing is that it's a selfish activity. Certainly it's a solo activity, in the sense that the only requirements are a surfer, a board and a wave, but that's not quite the same thing.

Sure, whether you call it stoke or buzz or pure exhilaration, surfers are all chasing the same good feeling, and yes, in pursuit of that feeling some may behave selfishly. However, that behaviour is only a reflection of the individual surfer – the act of surfing itself is no more inherently selfish than dancing or enjoying art or listening to music.

One word that crops up again and again in the stories in this book is 'community' – it recurs some 25 times, in fact, in the version I'm currently working on. Sometimes it's used to refer to a group of surfers in a particular area (see Laura Maynard's paintings of the 'Lewis surf community'); sometimes it's used to refer to the wider surf community of Scotland; and occasionally it's used in the context of the global community of surfers, now millions strong. What's clear, though, is that surfing is a force that brings people together rather than something that pushes them apart, and once you become a surfer, whether you realise it or not, you become connected to the same well of shared experience that unites wave-riders everywhere.

These connections don't always manifest themselves explicitly, but that doesn't make them any less powerful. In fact, the most subtle interactions can sometimes be the most telling. Which is where the title of this book comes in.

Imagine you've just ridden a wave to shore, and you're now paddling back out in search of the next one. As you move into deeper water, you see another surfer catch a wave, hop to their feet and come flying down the line towards you. You adjust your course slightly to make sure you don't get in their way, and as you pass over the shoulder of the wave they're on, perhaps just a few metres in front of them, you take a quick glance in their direction.

During this magical, paradoxical moment, the surfer you're looking at is moving both towards you, along the wave, but also away from you, towards the shore. Perhaps that's why, just for that instant, they seem to be frozen in time and space, moving-but-not-moving.

Sometimes you'll hear people enjoying this view from the shoulder give an encouraging hoot as the incoming surfer goes hurtling by; sometimes you might see them raise both arms to the sky in a moment of shared enjoyment. Often, though, a simple smile can be enough, a smile that says 'I see you, I get you, I know all about the journey that's taken you to this point, because I've been on that same journey too – or, at least, a version of it – and right now I'm as stoked for you, riding that wave, as if it was me up there, experiencing the glide.'

In a sense, then, this book is a series of views from the shoulder – a celebration of some incredible individual achievements, but also a celebration of the fleeting moments of connection which bind the surfing tribe together, both here in Scotland and far beyond.

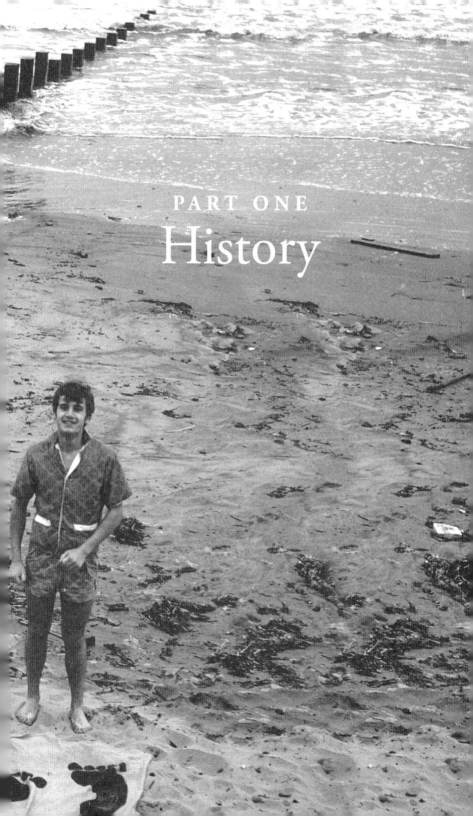

PART ONE
History

Previous pages: George Law (left), Andy Bennetts and Stuart Crichton
(right-hand page) at Aberdeen Beach, September 1968
(Courtesy of Andy Bennetts)

In search of a pioneer: Will the real Sandy Mathers please pick up?

LEARNING to surf can be tricky at the best of times, but for a group of teenagers trying to unlock the secrets of the ancient Hawaiian art in the waves breaking off Aberdeen Beach in the 1960s, it was made even harder by the flawed equipment they were using. Sandy Mathers and his friends, who had leaky plywood surfboards built for them by a local carpenter according to a pattern they found in a boys' magazine, were among the first people to surf in Scotland. At the start of each session the boards didn't work too badly, but gradually, as they started to fill up with water, they became more and more likely to sink nose-first on take-offs, catapulting their riders head-over-heels into the North Sea. The longer you surfed, the more difficult it became to catch a wave – not just because the boards became more likely to nose-dive as they took on more water, but because nobody in this early Scottish surf tribe owned a wetsuit, so the cold soon took its toll.

I might never have found out about the early misadventures of Mathers and his friends Graham Carnegie, Brian Morgan and Dave Killoh if I hadn't travelled to Aberdeen in the summer of 2006 to see an exhibition on the history of surfing in the UK at the city's Maritime Museum. Mathers & Co didn't feature in the show – at least, not officially. Curated by Paul Robinson, director of the British Museum of Surfing in Devon, the display of old boards, wetsuits, photos and other artefacts mostly focused on England and Wales, but there was a small section on Scotland, where it was claimed that the first people to surf north of the Border were an Englishman called Tris Cokes and an Australian called Graham Sorensen, who had travelled up from Cornwall in 1968.* Flicking through the comments in the visitor's book as I was about to leave, however, I spied an intriguing entry: 'Brings back memories. Surfed pre-68 in Aberdeen.' It was signed 'Sandy Mathers'.

This was a period when journalists were generally granted much more time and freedom to research and write stories than they are now, so when I returned to *The Scotsman's* former offices on Holyrood Road in Edinburgh, just across the street from the then newly-completed Scottish Parliament, I was able to spend what now seems like an almost comically disproportionate amount of time working my way through the Aberdeen phone book, calling every Alexander Mathers in the 01224 area to ask if they'd surfed back in the 60s. Most of my inquiries were met with polite bemusement, but eventually I struck gold, and the real, surfing Sandy Mathers picked up the phone.

After I filed the feature I'd been asked to write on the Aberdeen exhibition and the history of Scottish surfing more generally, all the details Mathers gave me about the sinking surfboards he and his friends rode were evidently cut from my copy. Still, Mathers, Carnegie, Morgan and Killoh did at least make it into the final piece. Photographer Simon Price was even tasked with taking a group portrait of these intrepid pioneers, and they ended up as the main image across a double page spread – rightful (albeit fleeting) recognition of their place in the story of Scottish surfing.

---

* Some have questioned whether Cokes made this journey in 1968, or at a later date, based on the style of board he appears to be riding.

8 July 2006

Scotland isn't renowned for its rich surfing history. When some of the best wave riders on Earth travelled to Thurso earlier this year to compete in the inaugural O'Neill Highland Open, the rest of the surfing world seemed to think it was hilarious. In its coverage of the contest, the Australian newspaper the Gold Coast Bulletin joked about the 'icy waters' of the Pentland Firth and described Scotland as 'a country best known for kilts, bagpipes and stuffed sheep's guts'. But perhaps the Aussies shouldn't have been so quick to have a laugh at our expense. As a new exhibition at the Aberdeen Maritime Museum shows, Scottish men and women were surfing years before their Antipodean cousins even knew what a surfboard looked like.

Peter Robinson is curator of the British Museum of Surfing, a not-for-profit organisation based in Braunton, Devon, and the man behind a new touring exhibition entitled The History of British Surfing. He firmly believes that Scots may have been surfing in the Hawaiian islands at the beginning of the 19th century, if not before. 'Quite a few Scottish people settled in Hawaii not long after Captain Cook had first made contact with the islands in 1778,' he says. 'There is a story of a chap – a Scotsman – arriving there on a boat in the early 1800s and expecting to be the first white man to settle, but he saw this white face in one of the outrigger canoes, paddling out with the natives to greet him, and when he spoke this fellow had a broad Scottish accent, so he'd been beaten by quite a few years. If this guy was in one of the outriggers with the locals, he would certainly have ridden waves in on the canoe, so you have to speculate that a Scotsman could have been one of the first non-Hawaiian people to surf.'

We will probably never know whether or not this anonymous Scottish settler had been introduced to the sport of surfing as well as the art of paddling an outrigger canoe. However, we can be absolutely certain that a Scot was surfing at Waikiki in the 1890s – more than two decades before the great Hawaiian surfer and swimmer, Duke Kahanamoku, first introduced surfing to Australia in 1915. Princess Victoria Ka'iulani Cleghorn – the first known Scottish surfer – was born in Honolulu in 1875 to Princess Miriam Likelike, sister to the reigning monarch of Hawaii, King David Kalakaua, and a Scotsman called Archibald Scott Cleghorn, a prosperous businessman, horticulturist and eventual governor of Oahu. Because she was second in line to the throne after Princess Lili'uokalani, her elderly and childless aunt, it was predicted that the young girl would eventually become queen of her country, and so in 1889, at the age of 13, Victoria was sent to England to receive a private education which would, it was hoped, prepare her for her future role as the head of a modern Hawaiian state.

Ka'iulani attended Great Harrowden Hall in Northampton-shire, and during her school years she also visited Brighton and Dreghorn Castle just outside Edinburgh, then the home of a Scots-Hawaiian plantation owner called Robert MacFie. However, in 1891 the Hawaiian monarchy was seriously weakened by the sudden death of Kalakaua. Lili'uokalani took the throne and named the young Ka'iulani as her heir, but she was forced to abdicate by a group of American investors, backed up by marines. In desperation, Ka'iulani toured Europe and the United States, campaigning to have the Hawaiian Royal Family reinstated, but her efforts were in vain, and by the time she returned to Hawaii in 1897 the monarchy had been abolished and the islands had become a republic. The following year, while out horse-riding, she was caught in a storm and came down with a fever. Her health never recovered, and she died on 6 March, 1899 at the age of 23.

These days, Ka'iulani is mainly of interest to historians because of her role as a figurehead for the Hawaiian independence movement, but she was also a skilful surfer.

The centrepiece of the exhibition at Aberdeen Maritime Museum is a replica of one of Ka'iulani's surfboards, lovingly hand-crafted out of solid koa wood by a Hawaiian shaper called Tom Pohaku Stone. Nicknamed Alihilani, or 'the heavenly horizon', it is a beautiful thing – a little over seven feet long and extremely thin, even by the standards of today's slender competition boards. 'The princess actually had two surfboards,' says Robinson. 'One was a big olo board – they could be anything up to 20 feet long. She would have ridden that in the big rolling combers. The other was a shorter board. Those were for more expert surfers, and were ridden in more critical waves, the kind of waves that a modern-day surfer would ride a shortboard on. So she was a really expert surfer – one of the old school of surfers at Waikiki and one of a dying breed at the time.' Is it possible that Ka'iulani could have surfed in Britain? 'We don't know yet, is the honest answer,' says Robinson. 'There's a quote about her from when she was living in Brighton about how she loved being "on the water again", and at the time Brighton was the sea-bathing capital of Britain, so there is a chance, but we haven't found anything yet that proves it one way or the other. I like to think she did.'

Ka'iulani might have surfed in Brighton or she might not, but Robinson is adamant that she never surfed on her visits north of the Border. According to an information panel in the exhibition, the first person ever to ride a wave in Scotland was Tris Cokes, in the summer of 1968. Now 56, Cokes runs a company called Homeblown in Redruth, Cornwall, which makes the foam blanks that surfboard shapers sculpt into surfboards. In the true spirit of a Sixties survivor he claims not to remember much about the summer of 1968, but when pushed he admits that it was the promise of romance – not surfing – that caused him to travel to Aberdeen. 'I'd met a girl down here in Cornwall during the summer,' he says, 'and she enticed us up there – myself and an Australian buddy called Graham Sorensen, who was living with me at the time. We'd come via Yorkshire, where we knew for sure there were waves, and then carried on up to her place and found a few around there as well.' There is a photograph of Cokes surfing at Aberdeen in the British Surfing Museum's archives, but it's difficult to deduce much from it. What were the conditions like that day?

'Hey – I'm 56 years old,' he says, 'I'm supposed to remember what the day was like 40 years ago? It was bloody cold in the water, I remember that.'

Thanks to the wonders of modern wetsuit technology, it's now possible to surf Aberdeen's waves all year round in relative comfort. By contrast, Cokes and Sorensen wore old-style 'beavertail' wetsuits, which only covered the upper body, leaving their arms and legs exposed to the chilly North Sea. The board they used was a 7'6" single-fin shaped by a New Zealander called Mooney, since deceased. Cokes isn't exactly sure which bit of beach they surfed in Aberdeen, but he remembers 'a jetty to the side of us'. According to Gordon Forbes, who runs Granite Reef surf shop in Aberdeen, this means it was probably a spot now known to local surfers as Footdee (pronounced 'Fittie'), which lies just to the south of the Harbour Wall.

However, it seems as if someone might have surfed in Aberdeen before Cokes and Sorensen. A note in the visitors' book at the Maritime Museum reads: 'Brings back memories. Surfed pre-68 in Aberdeen.' It is signed 'Sandy Mathers'. A phone around all the Alexander Mathers in the Aberdeen area reveals an Alexander

I Mathers of Bridge of Don, now 58, who says he surfed in Aberdeen in the summer of 1966, along with his friends Graham Carnegie, Brian Morgan and Dave Killoh. 'Graham and Brian had boards made in Aberdeen,' he says, 'wooden boards made to a plan that they had got in a magazine. The first time we went out we only had one board – eight-foot-plus it would have been – and we took turns. I can't remember who got the first shot, but I presume it would have been either Brian or Graham. The waves weren't that big, but sufficient to give it a go. Maybe a couple of feet.' Sadly, surfboard technology in the 1960s wasn't as advanced as it is today, and the historic board they rode in the summer of '66 fell to pieces years ago. Where did they surf? 'Just outside where the cafes are – we were always posers,' he laughs. Did they often get an audience? 'Oh yes, if you ever spoke to anyone up in Aberdeen, they all knew about the guys surfing and skateboarding on the prom. "Is it cold?" That was always the first question.'

The surfing craze soon spread to the rest of Scotland. In 1968, the same year that Cokes and Sorensen made their pilgrimage to Aberdeen, a student at Edinburgh University called Andy Bennetts saw people surfing while on holiday in Newquay and decided to give it a go in Aberdeen on his return. Not long after that, another pioneer, Willie Tait, took to the waves off Fraserburgh after bringing a surfboard home from a visit to California.

A Kiwi called Bob Treeby discovered the wealth of world-class waves breaking on Scotland's north coast in 1973, but it wasn't until 1976 that Angus Lamond Macnie unlocked the almost unlimited surf potential of the Hebrides, using a single-handed sailing vessel called the Sgian Ban, specially adapted for surf exploration. 'One of the great virtues of Sgian Ban,' he remembers, 'was that she could be sailed round a headland to find a great wave breaking, be anchored outside the break, the surfboard unhitched and off I'd go to enjoy the waves before returning to the craft and sailing or paddling onwards.'

Today, surfing in Scotland is fast becoming a mainstream sport. Exact figures are hard to come by, but according to one recent estimate there are more than 2,000 regular surfers in the Central Belt alone.

Prince William boosted the sport's profile when he learned to surf in St Andrews while at university there, and, following its initial success, it now looks as if the O'Neill Highland Open is going to become a regular fixture. Princess Victoria Ka'iulani Cleghorn – patron saint of Scottish surfers – would have approved.

How Pat Kiernan pitched Scotland's best wave to the world

IF THERE'S one surf spot in Scotland that you can be sure overseas surfers will have heard of, it's Thurso East. A north-west-facing reef break lying just outside Thurso harbour, in the right conditions it can produce powerful, perfectly peeling right-hand waves, and between 2006 and 2011 it played host to a series of professional surf contests, exposing it to the world's surfing media like never before. As a result, Thurso is now very much on the international surfing map, and these days the locals often find themselves in the water alongside itinerant surfers from far-flung locations. There was a time, though, when the place was still under the radar – so under the radar, in fact, that its one regular surfer got sick of surfing it all by himself, and decided to put out an SOS, inviting others to come and join him. Unthinkable now, but in the late 1970s all Liverpudlian Pat Kieran wanted to do was share the stoke.

7 May 2011

'Help!' reads the letter. '1 OR 2 SURFERS WANTED TO SHARE PERFECT RIVERMOUTH BREAK. 6–12ft. GLASSY PEELING USUALLY OFFSHORE AT THIS TIME OF YEAR. LOCATION: NORTHERN SCOTLAND. ACCOMMODATION: DOSSING SPACE IN COTTAGE OVERLOOKING BREAK.' Bashed out on a typewriter with a dodgy ribbon, and with 'CHRISTMAS 1978' scribbled at the top in Biro, Pat Kieran's note to the Northwest Surf Club in his native Liverpool doesn't look like anything special. But as relics of Scottish surfing history go, it's the equivalent of the Turin Shroud or Ark of the Covenant – a time capsule that, for the faithful, is loaded with meaning.

At the time it was written, hardly anybody in the surfing world had heard of Thurso; it simply wasn't on the map. Kieran, a keen surfer, had moved there in 1976 to take up a job at the Dounreay nuclear power plant, and was surprised and delighted to discover a world-class wave – Thurso East – breaking just a stone's throw from his house. Trouble was, he hardly had anybody to surf it with, so he decided to get his typewriter out and see if he could attract a few like-minded visitors.

I first clapped eyes on Kieran's historic missive two years ago, when it formed part of an exhibition of local surfing memorabilia at Caithness Horizons – the visitor centre now occupying the building that used to be Thurso Town Hall. Sitting in a display case surrounded by grainy photos of surfers in the bulky wetsuits of yesteryear, it looked like something from the impossibly distant past. It read like something from a bygone era, too. I remember being particularly amused by the line specifying that potential visitors 'MUST APPRECIATE PEACEFUL SURROUNDINGS

WITH VERY LAID BACK INHABITANTS'. The exhibition was held during that year's O'Neill Coldwater Classic surf contest, and as I read those words, less than a mile up the road a couple of hundred professional surfers, photographers and assorted hangers-on were swarming all over the very reef about which Kieran had waxed lyrical. Thurso East may have been peaceful in 1978, but it could hardly have been described as such in April 2009. Paradise lost or gained, depending on your point of view.

Kieran's letter also finds its way into Chris Nelson's excellent new book *Cold Water Souls*, an exploration of the way the sport of surfing has spread from its warm-water genesis points to more frigid corners of the world. There's a whole chapter devoted to the development of surfing in Scotland, and Nelson has done the Scottish surf community a huge service by filling in some of the blanks in what, up until now, has been a sparse narrative. After a nod to Alexander Mathers and his Aberdeen buddies, identified as among the first people ever to surf in Scotland, in the summer of 1966, and to Andy Bennetts and Willie Tait, who pioneered surfing around Edinburgh and Fraserburgh respectively, Nelson concentrates on the north coast. He talks to Grant Coghill, born and raised in Thurso, who took up a job at Dounreay straight after graduation. Coghill learned to surf from a mysterious, itinerant Kiwi called Bob Treeby who 'materialised' on the north coast in the early Seventies. Although Treeby gave lessons in the gentle rollers of Dunnet Bay, he kept his own favourite spots close to his chest. 'We didn't actually know where Bob went to catch his own waves,' says Coghill.

Elsewhere, there's a laugh-out-loud funny interview with many-times Scottish Champion Sheila Finlayson, in which she describes trying to learn to surf in the barrels of Brims Ness with pals from school in the early 1980s, after being inspired by an

Old Spice ad on TV. The best bits, though, are the glimpses of what life was like for Kieran and fellow pioneer Kevin Rankin in the late Seventies. At one point, Kieran reflects on his letter of 1978 and laughs. 'Today, at Thurso East, I'd say there's hardly a good wave that goes unsurfed now. You certainly couldn't say that back then.'

Neva MacDonald-Haig and the coffin-lid surfers of Machrihanish

WHO were the first people to surf in Scotland? That really depends on how you define 'surfing'. The first person to master the art of trimming across the face of an unbroken wave was probably Aberdeen surfer George Law in the mid-1960s and there is certainly early video footage of him doing so. But did people attempt to ride waves in Scotland before him? Yes, as it turns out, long before – as early as the 1930s, in fact. True, these early wave-widers may not have been able to fly along in the curl as Law did, but they were definitely riding the whitewater lying down, in which case they may well have been Scotland's first bodyboarders. And if one of them managed to scramble to their feet while being propelled shorewards, if only for a moment? Well – technically that would be surfing, albeit surfing of a pretty basic kind.

In the autumn of 2014 I received an email from a relative of Neva MacDonald-Haig, then 90 years old, who asked if I'd like to interview her about her time as one of the 'coffin lid surfers of Machrihanish'. As it turned out, Neva's brother Peter may or may not have been the first person ever to ride a wave in Scotland while standing on a surfboard – or, at least, something approximating a surfboard. Neva herself couldn't remember for certain if he'd ever managed to stand up or not, and the picture she sent me showed him in an ambiguous half-crouch, somewhere between standing and sitting. Either way though, it was clear from our conversation that Neva's childhood memories of west coast wave-riding meant a great deal to her, and that she enjoyed revisiting them in her later years.

8 November 2014

Up until last Thursday, I was fairly certain that the first people to surf in Scotland were either Sandy Mathers and his friends Graham Carnegie, Brian Morgan and Dave Killoh, who were teenagers when they started riding wooden surfboards in Aberdeen in 1966, or George Law, who first took to the waves off Aberdeen at around the same time, and who died earlier this year. Now, though, after speaking to one of the coffin-lid surfers of the Mull of Kintyre, I'm not so sure.

Neva MacDonald-Haig (née Gordon-Dean) of Drumnadrochit will just have turned 91 by the time you read this, and it's possible that her older brother, Peter Gordon-Dean, was the first person ever to surf in Scottish waters. MacDonald-Haig says that every summer from 1933 until about 1938, her parents Horace and Helen took her and her siblings Peter, Margaret and David on holiday to Westport, seven miles north of Machrihanish.

'There was this wonderful beach and never a soul on it except us,' she says. 'There's a picture of us all in our swimming clothes standing beside a sign that says this beach is dangerous for bathers' – but there was no talk about surfers. 'My father stood with us beside the sea one day and we were admiring and listening to the thunder of these great Atlantic rollers and he said to us,

"You know, there's nothing between us and America." We used to try and ride the waves with our bodies but he said "I think we should get help to ride these waves" and he went to the local undertaker. Now, it makes a good story to say they were coffin lids that we rode on but it's an exaggeration, they weren't really. The undertaker made these boards for us. I don't remember his name, I'm afraid, but we've got one or two pictures of us actually in the surf using these boards. The modern surfboards are all pointed aren't they? But these surfboards were rounded. The photos aren't very clear but you can see the shape. They were probably about five or six-feet long.'

The million dollar question for purists, of course, is: did anybody ever try to stand up on one of these undertaker-designed wave-riding vehicles? And did anybody succeed? Lying flat on a surfboard to ride a wave to the shore really counts as bodyboarding, and the identity of Scotland's first bodyboarder is perhaps a question for another time. MacDonald-Haig explains that she and her siblings mostly rode waves lying down, but there is one image in which her brother Peter certainly seems to be standing on his board, or at least trying to. It would certainly be possible to ride a pre-broken wave standing up on a board that length, although probably not for very long. It's hard to tell from the pictures, but the boards seem to have been little more than flat planks of wood, so they would probably have had to be moving quite fast before they were stable enough to stand on for any length of time.

Of course, it doesn't really matter whether Scotland's waves were first ridden by a stand-up surfer in the 1930s or the 1960s. The important thing is that we have plentiful waves on three coasts and have now figured out how to enjoy them, just as Neva MacDonald-Haig and her family did all those years ago. The same cottage we stayed at every year is still there,' she says, 'and it's now occupied by a surf instructor. We went to his house and he was very interested to hear this story. It's strange there now, with Westport car park and all the notices about surfing up. When we were there there was just . . . nothing. But to us it was heaven.'

First contact: Andy Bennetts and George Law's Aberdeen encounter

AT AROUND about the same time that Sandy Mathers and his pals were taking it in turns to get half-drowned by their hollow wooden surfboards up in Aberdeen, another group of young Scottish surfers decided to hit the waves in the Granite City. Ironically, Andy Bennetts, Ian Wishart and Stuart Crichton were based in Edinburgh, and – had they known where to look – could easily have found countless high-quality surf spots much closer to home. Having lived in Aberdeen for a time, however, Bennetts knew for certain that there were waves there, and so in September 1968 the three students took the train north together. They had just the one surfboard between them – a factory made board or 'pop out' Bennetts had acquired on a holiday to Cornwall – and, of course, no wetsuits.

When they arrived in Aberdeen, the trio thought they might be the only surfers in town – perhaps even the only surfers in Scotland. However, they were surprised to run into local surfer George Law, who had been riding waves there since 1967, taking advantage of the antisocial shift patterns at the abattoir where he worked to maximise his time in the water. Half a century on from their Aberdeen trip, I met up with Bennetts and Wishart in Shackleton's Pub in Edinburgh to hear more about this key moment in Scottish surfing history. Also present was Bill Batten, another pioneering Scottish surfer who had been surfing in south-east Scotland since 1967 and who, along with Bennetts and Wishart, soon became part of a small but dedicated group of surfers hunting for waves along the coast of East Lothian and down into the Scottish Borders.

18 August 2018

On 2 September this year, it will be the 50th anniversary of Scottish surfing's big 'Doctor Livingstone, I presume' moment – the day when surfers from Edinburgh first met up with surfers from Aberdeen, thereby forming the first known link between two of the nation's early, geographically isolated wave-riding tribes and laying the groundwork for what would eventually become a distinctive national surfing culture, with its own legends, its own contests and its own 'we-know-it's-freezing-but-we-don't-care' attitude. To mark the occasion, I caught up with three veterans of those pioneering days – Andy Bennetts, Ian Wishart and Bill Batten. Bennetts and Wishart were both on the much-discussed trip to Aberdeen in 1968, while Batten subsequently had a Doctor Livingstone moment of his own.

When they caught the train from Edinburgh to Aberdeen in early September 1968, teenagers Andy Bennetts, Ian Wishart and their friend Stuart Crichton were obsessed with Americana – as many people their age would have been one year on from the Summer of Love – and, armed with a surfboard owned by Bennetts, they also suspected that they might be the only surfers anywhere in Scotland. 'The surfing thing came about because Ian and I were both interested in cars and things American generally,' says Bennetts, 'drag racing, the Beach Boys – all that kind of stuff. We were going to university and we had a short holiday between the end of school and the start of university and we thought, because I had bought a surfboard at that point, let's go to Aberdeen, because I used to live there and I knew there were waves up there. The other chap was Stuart Crichton, who was also at school with us. We took my board which was a 9'6' pop-out [a factory-made surfboard] onto the train, got to Aberdeen, and then walked from the station carrying said board all the way to the beach, which was two miles maybe, something like that.'

'We got some funny looks,' remembers Wishart, 'people wondering what it was. We walked right down Union Street, right down Beach Boulevard all the way to the Beach Pavilion, which is no longer there – it was knocked down many years ago.'

'We got to the beach fully expecting our surfboard to be the only one around,' says Bennetts, 'and we thought well, we're not walking back and forth with this all the time so let's try and find a place to store it. We asked the guy in charge of the pavilion if we could leave the board somewhere and he said "put it in beside this other one" – at which point we were somewhat deflated, because George Law had been surfing there for a year before, and his board was kept permanently at the beach.'

Law, it turned out, had been surfing the waves off Aberdeen since 1967, his early shifts at a nearby slaughterhouse freeing him up to surf all afternoon. Bennetts and Co soon met up with him, and the four spent the next few days surfing together. 'Being poor prospective students,' says Bennetts, 'we didn't have the money to buy wetsuits, so it was on with the trunks and into the September Aberdeen sea.'

'It was very cold,' remembers Wishart,' but the caretaker of the pavilion was a nice chap who took pity on us because we were coming out frozen – he had a wee wood-burning stove and we sat around that.' Bennetts picks up the story: 'George Law just had a vest made of neoprene – he didn't have a proper wetsuit – and he'd been surfing there right through the winter, which in Aberdeen is quite some feat.'

Law only stayed on in Aberdeen for a couple more years before emigrating to Canada. He passed away in 2014, but he certainly left an indelible mark on the sport, and not only because of his historic meeting with Bennetts, Wishart and Crichton. In 1968, California's Surfer magazine, the Bible of the sport, ran an article about Scottish surfing – perhaps the first ever – based on an interview with Law, which began with the immortal words: 'Scotland??? Whoever heard of any surf in Scotland? Well, Scotsman George Law reports there's fine surfing off Aberdeen beach in the chilly North Sea.'

Once Bennetts, Crichton and Wishart were back in Edinburgh it didn't take them long to figure out that there were also plenty of places to surf closer to home, first in East Lothian and then further down the A1 – and before long, the surfing tribe of south-east Scotland started to attract new members. 'There were a few people [in Edinburgh] by this time with surfboards,' says Bennetts, 'and one of them was a guy called Pete Rennie. Pete didn't have a driving licence but his father was very sympathetic so he would give Pete and his board and me and my board a lift down to the beach. We were looking at Dunbar, Belhaven, round about that area. One day we were going to the beach and this van was coming up the other way with a board on the top. So we screeched to a halt, and it turned out to be Bill [Batten]. This was quite near Belhaven Bay. We asked him "where did you get that?" and he said, "Oh, New Zealand."'

'I'd surfed down the East Coast for a wee while before I met

Andy and Ian,' says Batten. 'My first time surfing in Scotland was December 1967. I was more or less there by accident. I'd lived in New Zealand, then Australia, and then I'd shipped a surfboard back. When it arrived somebody said to me, "Why don't you go to Pease Bay? I believe there are waves there." I said "That can't be possible," but I did go down, and the waves were reasonably big. The water was quite cold though, so I didn't stay in too long. I didn't have a wetsuit then, so it was shorts and in. Freeze, then get out quick.'

Unsurprisingly, Batten was inspired to get a wetsuit fairly soon after this first, bone-chilling experience. 'In 1968 I found a company [in Newquay] that sold neoprene rubber with draw-ings of how to cut out a wetsuit,' he says. 'It was more or less a diving wetsuit though, with a big flap at the front with buttons, and they sent you this neoprene and a plan and a tin of glue. So my wife and I spent a week cutting all this out and sticking it all together and that was my first wetsuit. Extremely uncomfortable but it was warmer than not having a wetsuit.'

As they started exploring further afield, the crew soon found that there were surf spots dotted all along the coast south of Dunbar. Bennetts picks up the story: 'We soon realised that Pease Bay had better waves than Belhaven – once you got your head around surfing over the rocks.'

'And Coldingham was almost a kind of a last resort,' adds Wishart. 'If Pease was closing out [too big to surf] then you could still get in at Coldingham, but Coldingham was a funny kind of break – it used to break right across the whole beach rather than giving you a decent ride.'

'You have to bear in mind that there weren't any decent weather forecasts,' says Bennetts. 'There certainly wasn't a swell forecast, so you went down on the basis of "It's Saturday, let's go down the beach."'

For all that Bennetts and Co pioneered many of the best-known spots in south-east Scotland, there were so few surfers in those days that once they'd found a few good ones there wasn't much incentive to keep looking. 'There were only 10 or 12 people total, so there wasn't the pressure to go and find somewhere else,' says Bennetts. That said, they did occasionally try surfing in different places just for the hell of it. Batten remembers one session at Dunbar that got him into trouble with the law. 'I surfed off the rocks at Dunbar once,' he remembers, 'where the harbour is – in the town itself. That wasn't a great idea because the police pulled me in and said, "What are you doing? We were about to send the lifeboat out for you!" I thought the lifeboat would probably have been wrecked, but I'd have been alright.'

No matter how good the waves on the east coast were, however, it was only ever going to be a matter of time before Scotland's surfers started looking west, to the powerful waves of the Atlantic. Travel times and costs being what they were in the late 1960s and early 1970s, the islands were a tricky proposition, but Machrihanish, on the swell-exposed southern tip of the Mull of Kintyre, was a little more accessible (although only a little), so it seemed like an obvious place to try. Although it can have great waves in certain conditions, Machrihanish and the spots nearby have a fairly narrow swell window so they can be maddeningly inconsistent, and in the days before accurate surf forecasts this made a trip there even more of a gamble than it is today. 'Machrihanish is relatively sheltered,' says Bennetts, 'so you didn't really know when you set off whether there were going to be waves until you got there.'

The next major discovery wasn't too long coming, however, and it was Batten who made it, stumbling upon the untapped surfing potential of Scotland's north coast completely by accident. 'I went to a wedding up there in about 1970,' he says, 'to a place called Bettyhill. I looked out of the window in the morning and these waves were rolling in and I thought, "Oh wow, this is the place to be!" I didn't have a board with me of course, but I did have a trip up there very quickly after that and that got the north shore going.' The now-famous barrels peeling along the reef at Thurso East weren't surfed until the mid-1970s, and they didn't really appear on the surfing world's radar until 1978, when Liverpudlian transplant Pat Kieran finally got lonely surfing them all by himself and wrote an article for an English surfing magazine appealing for people to come and join him.

In the early 70s, however, before Thurso became synonymous with surf, Batten, Bennetts, Wishart and Co found plenty of other great spots to keep them entertained around Bettyhill. 'Bettyhill was good because there was a choice of waves up there,' says Bennetts. 'You had Torrisdale, Farr Bay, Strathy . . . and nobody else had ever been up there [to surf] as far as we knew. The thing I remember about going up to Bettyhill was the drive,' he continues. 'You used to leave work [in Edinburgh] at four o'clock on Friday night and you drove for hours and hours and you got to Bettyhill at half-past 11, because there was no Kessock Bridge, it was the Kessock Ferry, and there was no Cromarty Bridge either. We took the single track road for the last bit from Helmsdale, by which time it was usually getting dark. So there would be three or four cars charging up this single track road, being aware of sheep . . .'

And that seems like as good a place as any to leave our three surfing pioneers, driving north through the lonely countryside of Sutherland as night falls, a little string of tail-lights following the winding course of the River Halladale towards the sea, and the promise of waves in the morning. Surfing, it is often said, is a sport that leaves no trace, but everyone who has surfed in Scottish waters since Bennetts, Batten and Wishart has been following in their footsteps, whether they realised it or not.

The remarkable surfing life of Iain Masson

IAIN Masson was a hugely significant figure in Scottish surfing, not just because of his formidable competitive record – seven national titles between 1990 and 1998 – but also because of the length of time he was able to continue surfing to a high level, and because of the many lives he touched during all those years spent in and around the water. When he died in early 2022, rather than trying to write a conventional obituary, I tried instead to pull together some of the many great stories about him by speaking to some of the surfers who knew him best.

The most surreal tale is Mark Cameron's yarn about the time he and Masson spent taxiing three-time world champion Tom Curren around the Isle of Lewis in 1991. Probably the most famous surfer on the planet at that time, having won his third world title in 1990, Curren was an unusually private, ego-free character in a sport typically dominated by big personalities. Perhaps in the offer of a trip to Lewis to take part in an experimental, low(ish) profile new contest, Curren saw the possibility of a brief respite from the glare of the world's surf media; and perhaps in Masson and Cameron he saw a couple of guys who, like him, didn't really care about the surf industry circus and just wanted to go surfing. One thing's for certain: if our lives are the sum of the stories we leave behind, then Iain Masson led a truly remarkable life.

12 February 2022

Scottish surfing lost one of its brightest stars earlier this month, when Iain Masson passed away at his home in St Combs in Aberdeenshire. A seven-time Scottish surfing champion, founder of the Point Northeast surf shop in Fraserburgh and a long-standing member of the town's Broch Surf Club, he died at home on 3 February with his wife Michelle by his side, following a lengthy battle with leukaemia. He was 56 years old.

Masson's legacy is huge. Not only did he dominate Scottish surfing in the 1990s, winning four national titles in a row from 1990–1993, then three more from 1996–1998, he continued to surf to a high standard until well into middle age. He first represented Scotland at the European Championships at Les Sables d'Olonne in France in 1987, and went on to become a fixture in the national team during the next three decades. Remarkably, in 2014 he was selected to represent Scotland at the World Surfing Games in Peru, making him the oldest competitor at the event at the age of 48.

Masson also played a major role in developing the infrastructure supporting surfing in Scotland. His friend and fellow Scottish surfing champion Malcolm Findlay credits him as the 'main driver' in bringing the British Surfing Championships to the east coast of Scotland for the first time, when they were held at Fraserburgh in 1995, and he was instrumental in resurrecting the Scottish Surfing Federation in the early 2000s, following a five-year hiatus. In addition, the Point Northeast surf shop which he ran with his friend Alan Wilson became a focal point for the Fraserburgh surf scene, and he also mentored several national champions.

One of his protégés was Mark Cameron, who won his own seventh Scottish title in 2016, making him the only surfer to equal Masson's record. 'Iain was a really quiet, easy-going guy,' says Cameron. 'I remember one day in particular going out for a surf with him as the wind dropped off and it was getting dark. I'm just the complete opposite to Iain, just a frantic maniac getting my suit on, boots on, but he's just nice and calm, having a wee stretch. I'm like "What are you doing man?!" But that was Iain – always very calm and collected.'

In 1991, Cameron and Masson travelled to the Isle of Lewis together to take part in an experimental surf contest set up by the free-thinking Australian surfer Derek Hynd. Disillusioned by the way the pro contests of the era seemed to kill creativity, Hynd had developed an innovative handicap system, allowing locals to compete alongside some of the best surfers in the world, notably three-time world champion Tom Curren. 'We drove from Fraserburgh to Stornoway and there was Derek Hynd and surfers like Hans Hagen and Frankie Oberholzer – it was just bizarre,' remembers Cameron. 'And then of course there was Tom Curren. He didnae really have any gear with him, didnae have any transport. We had quite a big camper van so he said "I'll just come and hang out wi' you guys" and so he'd come with us every day. I think he liked the fact that we weren't taking photos, didnae make a fuss. He was just like one of the boys. It was one of the coolest surf trips I've ever been on.'

Malcolm Findlay also has good memories of surf trips with Masson. 'At Aveiro in Portugal in 1989, five of us went down to the beach in a hire car that Iain was driving,' he remembers. 'As we sat checking whether the waves were worth the effort, a huge tipper lorry, loaded with boulders, began to reverse towards the car, slowly lifting its rear into tipping mode. Unfamiliar with the car and wrestling with the gearstick, Iain suddenly said "Ah canna find reverse!" He managed to reverse just in time to get clear, but the expression on his face was priceless when he turned around to share his relief and found himself alone in the car.'

Masson's influence is everywhere you look in Scottish surfing. Another Scottish champion, Mark Boyd, describes him as 'a true legend and inspiration to me as a young surfer. 'When I was a grom [during the Scottish Surfing Federation's hiatus] Iain was running some of the only surfing competitions in Scotland,' he says. 'He had a very smooth style and was incredibly consistent. His wave selection skills were second to none and he always had a knack of choosing waves which would allow for multiple manoeuvres. It was these competitions, and in particular watching Iain, that really made me want to improve and progress.'

Perhaps the last word should go to Andy Bennetts, one of the first people ever to surf in Scotland, a Scottish champion himself back in 1975, and probably the nearest thing Scottish surfing has to an official historian. 'My memories of Iain are simply that he was a really nice guy who didn't boast about his abilities,' he says. 'He was a great team player and although he surfed in South Africa and Australia, he always returned to the Broch, and was in the water there a great deal encouraging the youngsters. His death is a great loss to Scottish surfing.'

Vince Attfield and the origins of Scotland's northernmost surf community

IN A sense, the history of Scottish surfing is a process of various small, distinctive surf communities developing in isolation in different locations around the country, then slowly coalescing to form one multifaceted culture; and that story perhaps came to some sort of conclusion in the autumn of 2022, when the

Scottish Surfing Federation's Gathering of the Clans event took place in Shetland. The Clans is a good-natured team contest, bringing together surf clubs from all over Scotland to compete in longboarding and shortboarding divisions, with the best-performing team overall declared the winner. The event had never taken place in Shetland before – in fact, there had never been a surf contest of any description in Shetland before. However, as I discovered when I interviewed veteran Shetland surfer Vince Attfield, people had been surfing there since at least the early 1990s.

12 November 2022

Long-time Shetland surfer Vince Attfield is talking about the plentiful marine life he sees while riding waves at the various beaches, reefs and points near his home in Sumburgh. It's dolphins and porpoises mostly, he says, although he's also had a couple of encounters with 'whales' over the years. Is that 'whales' as in killer whales? 'Aye,' he says, 'orcas'. So how does he react when he suddenly sees one of those unmistakable fins knifing through the water? 'I just paddle in slowly,' he says. 'They say you're not supposed to panic when you see a shark, so I guess it's the same with an orca.'

Anyway, for surfers in this part of the North Atlantic, fearsome apex predators are fairly low down the list of day-to-day concerns. Public enemy number one is the wind. 'The surf here's pretty hit and miss,' says Attfield. 'Sometimes it can just be totally blown-out for days. The low pressures track straight across the Atlantic and usually end up right over the top of us, so it's only very occasionally that you'll get an offshore wind.' Last month, surfers from all over Scotland travelled to Sumburgh as the Scottish Surfing Federation held its annual Gathering of the Clans team contest in Shetland for the first time and – thankfully – the wind didn't spoil the fun.

Not only was this the first time the SSF had held a contest in Shetland, it was the first time there had been a surf contest in Shetland full-stop. Thurso's North Shore Surf Club took the title for the fifth consecutive year, with current Scottish champions Mark Boyd and Phoebe Strachan winning the two open divisions. However, the Shetland team, 60 Degrees North Boardriders, did themselves proud, with Joe Morton (Open Men), Peter Georgeson (Longboard) and Tom Wills (Masters) all making the finals in their divisions.

As president of 60 Degrees North Boardriders, Shetland's only surf club, Attfield played a key role in making the contest happen, helping to organise accommodation and using his local knowledge to decide where to hold the heats each day. In the end, the contest was held in two different locations: at a reef break called Boat Ramp on the first day and at the beach break at West Voe on the second. Both spots are close to Sumburgh, but there are plenty of other options in the area. 'The Boat Ramp is six minutes away from my house,' says Attfield. 'The nearest break's maybe two minutes away, and within less than ten miles there are maybe ten breaks, so there's not a lot of driving around. There are other breaks up in the north of the island and in the west, and then there's the outer islands, like Unst and Yell. If you're going there you make a day of it or even a weekend of it. I don't think there's anywhere in Shetland I've not checked yet. There are maybe one or two spots that have eluded me over the years but I think I've got most of them.'

Now 54, Attfield is originally from Fife, but moved to Shetland 32 years ago, where he works as an engineer. He's also pretty sure that he and two friends, Anthony Teart and Chris Jackson, were the first people ever to try surfing there, back in 1992. 'There was nobody surfing here when I started surfing,' he says. 'Me and my mates were coming back home drunk from the pub one night and we thought it would be a good idea to go surfing, so that's how it all kicked off. We could see the reefs at the end of the [airport] runway breaking on a beautiful moonlit night and we thought, "that looks pretty cool, we should maybe try surfing sometime." We made a surfboard out of plywood and expanded foam,' he continues, 'got a couple of Typhoon wetsuits, chucked ourselves in the water and got belted . . . and then it snowballed from there. We actually went to Quendell Beach first, so the Boatramp bay, but the shorebreak was pretty big and we didn't have a clue.'

These days, while there may be over 50 members of 60 Degrees North Boardriders, crowding still isn't much of an issue for Shetland surfers. Many of the people who belong to the club are only occasional visitors, Attfield reckons, and on a 'busy' day at one of the more popular breaks, there might only be six people in the water. When professional surf contests first started being held in Thurso on a regular basis in the mid-noughties, there was a fear that the waves there might suddenly be overrun by tourists, and numbers have increased. Are there now similar conversations happening in Shetland, in the wake of the SSF event?

'We've been speaking about this for years,' Attfield says, 'and we've always kept things pretty low-key here. But it costs so much to travel to Shetland, I can never see it really getting busy. I always tell people to come to Shetland to see Shetland,' he adds, 'because it's a beautiful place. Take a surfboard, and if you get waves, well, it's a bonus.'

PART TWO
Contests

Previous pages: Phoebe Strachan celebrates making the last eight of the women's longboard division at Eurosurf 2023 in Santa Cruz, Portugal (Malcolm Anderson)

Nuclear power: Big wave surfing in the shadow of Torness

THIS is the first story I ever wrote about surfing for *The Scotsman*. Although I was technically supposed to be working as an arts journalist at the time (and still am), writing 'across the paper' – outwith your supposed area of expertise – was encouraged. The outdoors pages in the *Scotsman Magazine*, published with the paper every Saturday, typically focused on more traditional outdoor pursuits like hillwalking, cycling and sailing, but evidently I managed to persuade the magazine editor Alison Gray to take a slightly improbable-sounding yarn about big wave surfing. Or, as it turned out, not so improbable. Sam Christopherson's planned Big Wave Challenge did indeed go ahead, when a big swell hit the east coast later in November, and so I headed down to the reef at Skateraw, just across the bay from Torness Nuclear Power Station, to watch him and a handful of others tackle grey, warbly, double-overhead waves.

I had hoped that I might be able to sneak a report on the contest into the sports pages, but unfortunately my write-up never made it past the sports editor's spike. The event certainly left an impression though: I still remember watching Sam and co paddling hard against the current flowing around the point to get back to the break after each wave, at times barely making any headway at all; still remember watching them flying around the headland, their bright contest jerseys the only splashes of colour in an otherwise dark, monochrome seascape. I remember the bitterly cold cross-offshore wind too; and I remember the very distinctive presence of the power station – not even in your line of sight as you looked out to sea from the tip of the point towards the surf, but somehow always there, making the whole event feel like some elaborate trespass, even though it was happening on a public beach.

I spoke to Sam many years after the contest took place and he said a guy came up to take part from somewhere in the north of England, had one quick look at the waves and went home again. Not big enough, apparently. Well, maybe it wasn't big-big – certainly not Hawaiian big – but it was still plenty big enough for most mortals, and the moody, slightly sinister setting cranked the intimidation factor up to 11.

12 November 2005

When most people think of big waves they imagine Hawaii or California – not the south-east coast of Scotland. But at some point between now and Christmas, conditions permitting, Dunbar-based surfer Sam Christopherson plans to stage the region's inaugural big wave surfing competition, the Big Wave Challenge. Open to men and women, the contest will be run on the first weekend in November or December with a swell of 8ft or more and favourable winds. The winner will receive a small cash prize and large dollops of respect from his or her peers.

Wave and wind patterns can be hellishly difficult to predict, but Christopherson, who has been surfing in the area for 15 years, says he's 'pretty confident' that the right conditions will materialise. 'The biggest waves we've ever surfed around here have been two-and-a-half times overhead – that's 15ft on the face,' he says. 'But there are only a couple of places that hold waves that big on our coastline, and most of the time they're a bit smaller.'

The most likely venues for the event are White Sands Beach near Dunbar and the daunting reef break at Skateraw, just next-door to Torness Nuclear Power Station. 'Skateraw's our big wave spot,' he says. 'It's the only place I've surfed at that kind of size and that I've seen work at that kind of size. The big days tend to be quite few and far between, but it tends to be November and December when it will break that big.'

Christopherson likens Skateraw to Mavericks, the fabled big wave spot at Half Moon Bay in California which claimed the life of surfing legend Mark Foo on an 18-to-20-foot day in 1994. Like Mavericks, the waves at Skateraw rear up out of deep water and break onto a shallow reef. The two spots also share the same menacing aura. An American surf journalist once described Mavericks as 'like Edward Scissorhands' mansion', and Christopherson talks of a similarly forbidding vibe at Skateraw. 'It's a sketchy place to be,' he says. 'Because you're next to the power station it feels like you shouldn't be there anyway, and when it's big there's lots of water moving about over a relatively uneven reef so you know if you don't get it right it can all go a bit Pete Tong.'

Christopherson learned to surf in Cornwall when he was 'really young'. Now 32, he runs the Coast to Coast Surf School in Dunbar, helping beginners ride their first waves at Belhaven Bay and taking parties of intermediate and advanced surfers to more challenging spots further afield. Coast to Coast also boasts Scotland's first junior surfing programme, which not only teaches children how to stand up on a board but also how to surf competitively. The goal is to produce surfers who can compete at both a British and international standard in years to come.

In spite of his efforts to bring on the next generation, however, Christopherson reckons there are only a handful of local surfers who will be able to handle a really big day at Skateraw.

'There are probably half a dozen guys who can handle big waves down here,' he says. 'If the swell's slightly smaller – maybe double overhead – then you could probably attract 20 to 25 surfers from down here. Much above that and I'm having to attract people from other regions. There are quite a lot of people up in Aberdeen and in Thurso who surf some solid waves up there, but it really depends on whether they want to make the journey down here.'

The format of the Big Wave Challenge will vary depending on what the waves are doing. If the conditions are epic, the prize money (the amount is still to be confirmed) will simply go to the best ride of the day. If the waves are smaller, however, there will be a conventional knockout competition, with surfers facing off in timed heats and receiving marks for the size of waves they catch, the length of their rides and the manoeuvres they perform.

Of the all the surfers Christopherson expects to enter the competition, three stand out as possible winners: 'One of the guys really charging down here is Damon Hewitt,' he says. 'He used to be a bodyboarder and he's still got that bodyboard mentality now that he's surfing, which is just: "go for it, over the falls, it doesn't matter". There are a few others – a guy called Euan Bruce is pretty good and so is Chris Cook. Outside those three, you're kind of hitting the next level down.' Giant surf can be a great leveller, though, so the Big Wave Challenge may yet throw up a surprise or two.

A Winter's tale: Cornishman Russ wins the first Highland Open

FOR many years, I used to carry a folded, dog-eared photograph in my wallet. The picture showed a beautiful, tapering, head-high wave at a surf spot on the east coast. Partly I kept it with me because it was a reminder of a good day's surfing. Mostly, though, it was there for when somebody said 'you can't surf in Scotland.' After years of trying to describe how good the waves could get to total strangers, I'd realised it was quicker and easier to simply show them that photograph. I can't remember exactly when I stopped carrying that snap with me everywhere I went, but I think it was probably sometime around 2006, when the first Highland Open surf contest was held on the north coast. Suddenly pictures of pros like Australia's Kieran Perrow, Hawaii's Love Hodel and Cornwall's Russell Winter riding perfect Scottish waves seemed to be everywhere. Point-proving wallet photos were no longer required.

13 May 2006

More often than not, surfing competitions are held at spots that don't really favour spectators. When the tide goes out at flat beaches like the one at Lacanau in France it can be impossible to see what's going on above the heads of the other people watching; scary reef passes such as Teahupo'o in Fiji look incredible if you're lucky enough to be sitting in one of the boats in the channel, but you can forget about trying to see any of the action from the beach.

Brims Ness, however, which played host to the final rounds of the O'Neill Highland Open earlier this month, is as observer-friendly a surf spot as you could wish for. Situated on Caithness's rugged north coast, just to the west of Thurso, it consists of a huge rocky slab jutting out into the treacherous waters of the Pentland Firth. Access isn't too tricky – you simply turn off the A835 and drive through a farmyard to get there. What really makes Brims a great place to watch surfing, though, is the shape of the reef itself. Because it shelves so abruptly, fast, hollow waves break only a few yards from dry land. Standing right at the water's edge, at times it feels as if you could reach out and high-five the surfers as they fly past.

The Highland Open, which ran from 25 April to 2 May, was a big deal for various reasons. For a start, the contest was the most northerly in the history of professional surfing, and easily the coldest. It was also rated a five-star event on the World Qualifying Series (WQS) – the competition that feeds directly into surfing's lucrative World Championship Tour (WCT), in which the best 45 surfers in the world battle it out for serious prize money at some of the most perfect surfing locales on Earth. Any surfer looking to make the grade for next year's WCT had no choice but to don an extra-thick wetsuit and go after the Highland Open's $12,000 (£6,500)/2,000 point first prize.

The early rounds of the contest were held at the reef break at Thurso East – another world-class surf spot nearby. Most of the British surfers were knocked out early, including local hero Chris Noble, arguably the greatest barrel-rider Scotland has ever produced. By the time the quarter-finals rolled around, Newquay's Russell Winter was the only Brit still in with a shout, after taking down the Brazilian WCT veteran Neco Padaratz in the fifth round. The contest had to be put on hold for a couple of days due to lack of swell, but on the whole the waves co-operated, and surfers from all over the world were impressed. Australian Kieren Perrow praised the 'amazing barrels' at Brims, while Hawaii's Love Hodel described the surf as 'just like back home'.

For the finals, Neptune really did the contest organisers proud, hurling solid overhead waves at Brims and sculpting them into snaking, smoking barrels with brisk offshore winds. In pro surfing contests, surfers can ride up to 10 waves per heat but are only scored on their best two rides, so the emphasis is on taking risks. The last eight didn't disappoint, pulling into tube after tube over the shallow reef. In the quarters, Winter bested Perrow, while on the other side of the draw Brazil's Bernardo Miranda upset the big-name American, Ben Bourgeois. Winter then won an incredibly close heat against Australia's Luke Munro to make the final, where he met Miranda, who had disposed of the promising young Basque surfer Aritz Aranburu in the other semi. Winter started slowly, letting Miranda take two scoring waves before he even got one. He soon found his stride, though. After putting himself back in contention with a solid score of 7.83, he proceeded to pull into a gaping, stand-up barrel for a perfect 10 to all but kill off the heat. Miranda battled valiantly, but in the end Winter held on for a comfortable win.

According to Bernhard Ritzer, a spokesman for the Highland Pro, there's every chance that Brims and Thurso East will feature on the WQS tour in years to come. 'I think we'll be back,' he says. 'We've already been checking some more spots down the coast – there are so many – all reefs. In future we can maybe use some more of the opportunities we have up here.'

When Sunny Garcia went barefoot at Brims

BY THE time the 2008 Highland Open rolled around, there was a concerted effort to invite journalists from mainstream media outlets, so rather than making my own way to the contest, I attended this one as part of a group of official media invitees. Train travel was laid on from Edinburgh, accommodation was provided at the Royal Thurso Hotel and a shuttle bus conveyed hacks to and from the contest site. All very pleasant. The only problem was, when I woke up bright and early on day one of the contest, the surfers were already on their way to Brims Ness to warm up but the first media shuttle wasn't leaving for a couple of hours. The thought of sitting in a hotel lobby twiddling my thumbs while some of the best surfers in the world rode one of Scotland's best waves just a few miles down the road was too painful to contemplate, so I grabbed my camera and started walking.

I'd only got a mile or so down the road when a passing driver took pity on me and offered me a lift. Just as well they did, because I'd only just made my way to the edge of the reef and set up my camera when Hawaiian legend and 2000 world champion Sunny Garcia paddled out – one of the most celebrated surfers in history dipping a toe in Scottish waters for the first time. His first wave wasn't bad, but the second one. . . well. . . for a wave like that to materialise at that precise moment, on what had up to that point felt like a small-ish day, it really did feel as if the ocean had suddenly realised that a significant surfer had entered the water and sent him a wave worthy of his reputation.

The only thing more surreal than watching Garcia ride that wave was being the only journalist on the reef waiting for him when he came in. In most of the world's major surf zones, he would have been mobbed by crowds of surf fans, all jostling to try and get him to sign a hat or a T-shirt. At Brims, though, it was just me waiting with a very hesitant 'Er, good morning Mr Garcia. . .' Not long after that, the PR who had been charged with corralling all the media types to the beach called, wanting to know why the hell I wasn't in the hotel lobby – the shuttle bus was due to leave in five minutes.

Beyond the presence of surfing royalty, the 2008 Highland Open was also notable for the brave display put on by Scottish wildcard

Mark Cameron in the first round. His last-ditch barrel attempt had the spectators on the shore holding their breath, and on a different day, with a fraction more luck on his side, it could have made him the first Scot to advance through a heat in a pro contest.

26 April 2008

'I'm gonna need some gloves, man,' says Federico Pilurzu, shivering at the thought of paddling out into the frigid waters of the Pentland Firth. Pilurzu, a Costa Rican, and his buddy Gony Zubizarreta from Spain, are browsing the racks at the Tempest surf shop, the focal point of the Thurso surf scene. From the outside, the Tempest may not seem like much – just a wooden shack with a corrugated iron roof – but it is stocked with everything a serious coldwater surfer could ever need, from boards and wetsuits to neoprene hoods, gloves and boots. Zubizaretta has surfed in Scotland before, so knows what to expect, but Pilurzu has never dipped a toe anywhere quite this chilly in his life. 'Back home I'm used to surfing in boardshorts,' he says. 'There, the biggest problem is protecting yourself from the sun.'

It's day one of the O'Neill Highland Open, the most prestigious surfing competition in the UK, and the coldest and most northerly on the pro circuit. Some 144 surfers have arrived from all over the world to battle it out for the $70,000 (£35,000) prize purse, but unfortunately there's no swell yet, not even a ripple, so most of them are milling around town, killing time. With their deep suntans and assortment of foreign accents, they're not exactly difficult to spot. In the foyer of the Royal Hotel, two women of a certain age break off their conversation about whether to have chips or boiled potatoes with lunch to watch a posse of bronzed American boardriders saunter past. In the town's main shopping precinct, two Aussie surfers exchanging loud 'G'days' draw quizzical looks from passers-by.

Not that the people of Thurso aren't happy about this influx of exotic young people to their town. On the whole, they seem delighted. Kay Rosie, owner of the Fish Bowl fish shop, has lived in Thurso all her life. She reckons surfers started making the pilgrimage here in significant numbers about 10 years ago, as word of the quality reef break at Thurso East started to spread. These strange new visitors certainly didn't hurt business in the town, but the advent of the Highland Open, in 2006, has had a real impact. 'The Open's great for the local economy,' she says. 'The cafes are busier, the hotels are busier and, of course, it's nice seeing lots of new faces in the town.'

It's estimated that the event is worth around £450,000 to Thurso every year, before even taking into account the positive impact it has made on the town's image. It is made possible by co-sponsors O'Neill, Swatch and Red Bull, who between them fund the event to the tune of £400,000. The owner of the Tempest surf shop, Helen MacInnes, has more reason to be cheerful about the Open than most. 'It's been like having two Christmases at once this year,' she says. 'I'd just like to say a big thank you to Terminal Five at Heathrow, because they've lost a lot of the surfers' stuff. Obviously it's a bummer for the surfers, but for me it's been the difference between [professional] life and death, because they're buying up all my wetsuits, boots and gloves.'

MacInnes has run the Tempest for four years, and during that time she's seen the attitude of Thurso's local surfers towards the contest change from initial suspicion to laid-back acceptance. 'The first year of the contest, there was a definite sense of panic,' she says. 'It was fear of the unknown. They didn't know if O'Neill were going to come up and completely expose Thurso – which has always been a bit of a secret – or if the contest was going to benefit the local surfing community. Most of them were falling on the side of "it's going to be a disaster". But once the [first] contest had been and gone, I think they saw it was a good thing. They sorted the car park out, and the event really inspired a lot of the local kids.'

The area around Thurso is blessed with some of the best surf spots in Europe, and because the Highland Open is a mobile contest, it is able to take advantage of all of them. Thurso East is the premier break in the area – a long, winding right-hander (a wave that breaks from right to left as you look at it from the beach) – that can be as good as anywhere in the world on its day. And then there's Brims Ness, a short, sharp shock of a wave a few miles to the west that's ideal for the purposes of a surfing competition in that it picks up almost any swell going.

Professional surfer Sam Lamiroy, one of only a handful of Brits in the event, sums up the differences between the two. 'Brims is like a really good Chinese takeaway,' he says. 'It's like a quick MSG hit, whereas Thurso East is more like an expansive, elaborate six-course meal with all the trimmings. They each have their place. If anything, surfing in the past few years has gone a lot more towards shallow slabs like Brims. Five or six years ago, a perfect wave was somewhere like Jeffrey's Bay in South Africa, which is a lot like Thurso East, but with the advent of places like Shipsterns Bluff [in Tasmania] and Teahupo'o [in Tahiti], people are looking more for these heavy, thick, barrelling waves, and that's where Brims Ness comes into its own.'

The surf has picked up. It's not huge – 'about shoulder high,' according to Lamiroy, just back from an early-morning surf check – but nevertheless the contest has been called on at Brims. Just before the competition gets underway, a little piece of surfing history takes place. Hawaiian legend and former world surfing champion Sunny Garcia takes to the water for a quick warm-up – his first ever surf in Scotland. The waves have been OK up to this point, but nothing to write home about. A few minutes after Garcia paddles out, however, some much bigger sets come rumbling through. It's almost as if Brims is saying 'welcome to Scotland' to one of surfing's favourite sons. On his first wave, Garcia carves a couple of tight, spray-flinging turns and, on his second he tucks into a sweet little barrel. One more wave and he's back on the beach, heading back to his hire car. Did he enjoy his first surf in Scotland? 'There are a couple of spots like this where I'm from, so this suits me just fine,' he says. 'I'm not afraid of the reef.' True to his hard-man image, Garcia isn't wearing wetsuit boots like everyone else. How's he coping with the cold? 'It's not too bad,' he says. 'The water's a little colder than I'm used to, but it's not as bad as I thought it was going to be. I can't wait to surf out here when it's a little bigger – I've seen the photos, so I know how good it can get.'

The competition eventually gets underway at 10:30am, and the first heat features the only Scottish surfer in the draw, Fraserburgh's Mark Cameron. In order to qualify for the Open, Cameron had to win the Scottish Championships earlier this month. He's entered only two competitions in the past three years, so he says he doesn't fancy his chances against touring pros who surf in contests week in, week out. As it turns out, though, he does his country proud. Heats at Thurso last for half an hour, and competitors have all the waves they ride scored out of ten by a panel of judges. They can surf as many waves as they want, but only their best two scores will count, so the pressure is on to 'go big or go home'. The most points are awarded to the surfer performing the most explosive manoeuvres in the most critical part of the wave – in other words, the guy carving big turns right under the falling lip should score more than the guy hopping around on the shoulder (the flat, safe part). Tube rides, or barrels, where the surfer rides inside a breaking wave, score highest of all.

Cameron is up against Jean Sebastien Estienne from France, Felix Messias from Brazil and David Mailman from the US. Estienne and Felix quickly move into first and second, with the Frenchman surfing particularly strongly. Only the top two surfers in the heat will progress to the next round, so Cameron finds himself playing catch-up. He nabs one or two decent rides, but with 10 minutes to go, he still needs a 5.5 score to move into second place. After a bit of a lull, he takes off on a solid six-footer, thinks about pulling into the barrel as the wave starts to hollow out in front of him but then opts to play safe and skate around the section. It's a great wave by normal standards, but the judges are not impressed, and he stays in third. With just a couple of minutes to go, another lump appears on the horizon. As the wave lurches onto the reef, Cameron hops to his feet, drops down its face and, this time, ducks under the lip. He's so deep in the tube that, if he makes it out, he should easily get into the next round. Sadly, though, Mother Ocean has other ideas: the wave shuts down and Cameron is slammed onto the almost-dry reef. At the buzzer he's still in third – out of the contest and left to reflect on what might have been.

Spin it to win it: Mark Cameron lands Nationals title with a 360

OF ALL the surfing competitions I've covered around Scotland, the 2009 Scottish National Surfing Championships is the one I remember most clearly – perhaps because it was so nearly a write-off. Come finals day, the waves were too small and inconsistent at both Thurso East and Brims Ness – the two customary north shore contest sites – and, with time running out, it seemed likely that the plug was going to be pulled on the whole shebang. I remember seeing contest organisers Chris Noble and William Watson standing at the edge of the reef together at Thurso, checking the small, grey, dismal-looking waves, weighing their options.

Their decision to travel half an hour west to Melvich may have seemed like an act of desperation at the time, but as it turned out it was inspired. The brown, peaty waves peeling across the mouth of the River Halladale were already looking good when we arrived, and they kept on getting better as the tide pushed in. There was some electric surfing from George Watt and eventual winner Mark Cameron, and relief all round that the event had been saved. Then, in the prize-giving ceremony at the local pub afterwards Noble – a past Nationals winner himself – gave a surprisingly emotional, heartfelt speech about what it means to get your hands on the coveted trophy, before handing it over to his old rival Cameron. It was the perfect ending to an unexpectedly perfect day.

18 April 2009

It is 1pm on the second and final day of the 2009 Scottish Surfing Championships, and the best surfers in the country are gathered in a farmyard-cum-car park, overlooking the reef break at Thurso East. In an ideal world there would be perfect, hollow waves spitting and reeling along this kelp-covered rock slab, but today: nothing. A few heats were held here early in the morning in smallish surf, but now the sea looks worryingly calm. Thurso East is Scotland's premier wave, but it only works in a big swell. There are other spots in the area which should be surfable under these marginal conditions, however, so contest director Chris Noble and his team are going to have to up sticks and transport their entire operation to a different beach. And with only a few hours to go until dark, and lots of heats still to run, they will have to move fast.

'I know this isn't what a lot of you guys are going to want to hear,' Noble tells the assembled competitors, 'but we're going to get this event finished today, even if it's in the ugliest waves you can imagine.' In years gone by, there wouldn't have been any great rush to crown a Scottish surfing champ, but times have changed. Since 2006, the Association of Surfing Professionals (ASP) has held a major contest in Thurso every spring – the O'Neill Highland Open – and offered a first round wildcard berth to that year's best Scots rider. With the 2009 pro contest just weeks away, the Scottish Surfing Federation (SSF) needs to select a representative to compete against the big boys, and soon, preferably today.

When the surf is too small for Thurso East, there are usually surfable waves at Brims Ness – a nearby reef open to the full force of the North Atlantic. The surf here is reported to be more powerful but also lumpy and unpredictable because it's exposed to the wind, so in the end Noble gambles and calls the contest on at Melvich – a beachbreak half an hour's drive to the west. Within seconds, a convoy of surf mobiles is bouncing out of the farmyard and heading for the coast road.

The arrival of the ASP event in Thurso in 2006 wasn't to everyone's liking. Sure, local surfers would get to see the best in the world riding their waves, but they would also have spectacular pictures of their favourite spots plastered all over the surfing media, potentially sending hordes of foreign surfers high-tailing it to the north coast of Scotland. At the SSF's AGM, held at the end of the first day of this year's Scottish Surfing Championships at Thurso's Tempest surf shop and cafe, the general consensus seems to be that the media feeding frenzy surrounding the ASP contest has definitely resulted in more crowded waves, but that the thing is here to stay, so the Scottish surfing community may as well try to get something out of it.

The SSF is keen to foster youth development. At one point it looked as if event sponsors, O'Neill, were going to get some of the pros competing in the 2009 event to put on masterclasses for young Scottish surfers at beaches all around the country, but now the humongous multinational retailer claims it no longer has the budget for such altruistic acts. Credit crunch or no, it would surely be a nice gesture – a way of putting something back into a surfing community that has, on the whole, welcomed the pro surfing circus with open arms.

Melvich is a beautiful surfing spot – a huge sweep of white sand – and it's a relief to see small but perfectly formed waves breaking in front of the rivermouth at its eastern end. As the tide pushes in, the waves get a little bigger until, by the time the four-man final hits the water, they're shoulder-to-head high and peeling into the river with machine-like precision. Fraserburgh's George Watt, 21, takes an early lead, surfing with real power and style. In the end, though, he is narrowly beaten by last year's champion, Mark 'Scratch' Cameron, 31, who pulls off a spectacular aerial 360 to clinch first place. 'I'm obviously delighted to have come out on top,' Cameron says, at an awards ceremony at the nearby Halladale Inn, 'particularly when such a good crew of surfers came up for the competition.'

Last year, Cameron narrowly missed out on causing a major upset in the first round of the Highland Open with a brave display of tube riding. Does he think he can do something similar this year? 'It's a great experience to come up here and see all the pro surfers,' he says. 'They're really good compared to me, so it boosts my surfing, having to compete with them. So, we'll see.'

Time travelling at the Belhaven retro board comp

THERE are various consistent, user-friendly surf spots within a short drive of Edinburgh, but Belhaven Bay near Dunbar is the closest to the city and, as a result, it tends to get crowded when the waves are good. In many countries in the world, the atmosphere in the water at busy, city-adjacent places like this can get toxic, often with those living closest to the break trying to intimidate those from further afield – something known euphemistically in the surfing world as 'localism'. Tactics range from having your car tyres let down and 'go home' written in surf wax across your windscreen to shouted threats and physical violence.

In all my years of surfing at Belhaven, though, (and I've surfed here a lot) I've never seen anything like this. Partly, the mellow vibe in the water is a function of the size of the beach – at about a mile long, there are usually multiple different sandbars working on a good day, so if one of them gets too crowded you can simply paddle over to the next one. Another big factor, though, is that the ethos of the local surf school, Coast to Coast, is unfailingly positive and inclusive. Hundreds, perhaps even thousands of people will have learned to surf at Belhaven with C2C over the years, under the instruction of local surfer Sam Christopherson and his team, and many of them will have become Belhaven regulars. The relaxed atmosphere, then, is also a tribute to them, and if any one event I've seen them put on over the years embodied their laid-back, good-humoured, let's-not-take-ourselves-too-seriously approach, it was this, the 2009 retro board contest which saw contestants goofing around on a range of vintage surf craft.

14 November 2009

Standing at the water's edge at Belhaven Bay near Dunbar the other week, I was reminded of Malibu Beach, California – and not just because the sun was beating down from a cloudless sky and the air temperature was hovering improbably around the 16C mark. This was the venue for a retro surf contest organised by local surf school Coast to Coast, and surfers of all ages were skimming across gently peeling waist-high waves, perched on the long, elegant surfboards of yesteryear. Most surfing contests these days feature serious-looking aquatic athletes riding almost identical short, pointy surfboards with three fins on the bottom. Known as shortboards or thrusters, these are the F16s of the surfing world, and they allow surfers at the top of their game to pull off spectacular, explosive manoeuvres in fast, hollow waves. In fact, it could be argued that the thruster represents the high-point of surfboard evolution: the basic design was created in the early 1980s by Australian shaper Simon Anderson and top surfers have been using it to win world titles ever since.

In the 1960s, though, when surfing had only just broken into mainstream culture, the surfing vehicle of choice was the longboard or Malibu board, named after the pointbreak of the same name, which had become the epicentre of the California surf scene. Over nine feet in length, usually with one fin on the bottom and wider at the nose than at the tail, these boards create a completely different surfing experience to the modern short-board. Whereas shortboards are set up to allow their riders to make tight, powerful turns, longboards are quite happy to travel in a more-or-less straight line, providing a stable platform on which the rider can perform tricks and stunts. These range from the balletic art of noseriding, which involves 'cross-stepping' to the nose of the board and hanging either five or ten toes over the end, to more comedic moves such as 'riding coffin' – lying down mid-ride and crossing your arms across your chest as if you're about to be buried.

Riding a longboard, then, is a way of tapping into a bygone age when surfing was all about goofing around and having fun, and the Coast to Coast retro comp perfectly reflected that vibe. The junior final was won by Clover Christopherson, daughter of Coast to Coast's head honcho Sam and at just seven years old almost certainly the youngest person ever to win a surfing competition in Scotland. Clover impressed the judges with her nonchalant poise in the curl and also with the length of her rides – her highest-scoring wave seemed to go on for about ten minutes.

The senior final, meanwhile, featured four very different surf-ers: Angus MacDonald has a beautiful, fluid style and seems to flow along waves with hardly any effort at all; Tim Christopherson, brother of Sam, is the exact opposite – a ferocious surfer who rides a longboard like most people would ride a shortboard, mak-ing sweeping, spray-flinging turns; Max Ferguson Hook, just 14 but already surfing better than most grown-ups, has an uncanny ability to generate speed from nowhere; while Sam himself is a true disciple of the old-school, with a dazzling repertoire of tricks at his disposal. MacDonald started strongly, tucking into the curl of a fast, reeling right-hander and then Ferguson Hook joined the fray with a swift right topped off with an attempted backwards nose-ride. In the end, though, it came down to a battle between the brothers Christopherson. Tim must have thought he'd won when he smacked one of the biggest waves of the day all the way to the beach and then backed it up by riding coffin on a perfect little two-footer. In the end, though, he narrowly lost out to Sam, who pulled off a headstand, screamed through the longest nose-ride of the day and then, for the piece de resistance, demonstrated an oddly pious take on the coffin ride, with his hands pressed together in silent prayer.

I visited Malibu a few years ago, and its golden age is long gone: it's far too crowded now, and as a result the atmosphere in the water can get downright unpleasant. Scotland may be colder, but it has some of the best waves in Europe and advances in wetsuit technology mean it's possible to surf them comfortably all year round. Our surfer population is still small, our best waves still go mostly unridden and total strangers still give you a friendly wave when you paddle out into the line-up. Our golden age is now.

How Chris Noble took on the pros and won

CHRIS Noble's first round heat win at the 2010 O'Neill Coldwater Classic at Thurso East was an important milestone for Scottish surfing. Previously, the Classic (formerly the Highland Open) had felt like something that happened to Scotland rather than with it. Sure, a local surfer or two might be granted a wildcard entry to compete against the professionals in the first round every year, but these amateurs were never really expected to present a significant challenge. However, the fact that Noble, who had to fit in his surfing around a full-time job, could take on and defeat two full-time pros, showed that Scotland's best surfers were no longer just there to make up the numbers.

With the benefit of hindsight, what's particularly impressive about this post-contest interview is that, far from basking in the glory of his achievement, Noble was already focusing on how Scottish surfing as a whole could progress, and in particular on the infrastructure needed for the next generation of Scottish surfers to succeed. At the time, I remember thinking that the idea of Scotland fielding a team at the ISA World Surfing Games seemed like something that might take place in some distant future. But, of course, that dream was only a few years away from becoming a reality.

1 May 2010

It is 8am on the penultimate day of the O'Neill Coldwater Classic, the international surfing circus that visits Thurso every spring, and local surfer Chris Noble is sitting in his van at the contest site at Thurso East, expertly demolishing a bacon and egg roll and dreaming big dreams for Scotland's wave-riding future. 'I was told a long time ago, "Oh, you're never going to have a professional surfer in Scotland – it's just not going to happen." But why not? At the end of the day we've got waves that are just as good as anywhere, and we can surf just as good as these guys.'

By 'these guys', Noble means professional surfers – the tanned 'n' toned army of aquatic athletes sponsored by multi-million dollar surf companies who tour the world's best surf spots year after year, desperately battling for the contest points and prize money that will allow them to go on living the dream. Up until a couple of days ago, his claim that the best Scottish surfers are at the same level as their itinerant brethren from Australia and Hawaii might have raised a few incredulous eyebrows; now, though, it's a proven fact.

On 14 April, Noble made surfing history when he became the first Scot to progress from the opening round of the Coldwater Classic since its inception in 2006. He didn't just sneak through his heat, either – he won it emphatically, getting barrelled to beat Brazil's Ricardo Dos Santos and Cornwall's Lyndon Wake. 'Things just sort of fell into place for me in that heat,' he says. 'Straight off the hooter I got a wave that never really did that much, but it let me see the standard of the guys I was surfing against because I got stuck on the inside for a wee bit. Then I got back outside and got another wave and got a cutback on it and thought "well, that was OK," and then I paddled back out and got a nice tube and took it from there.'

Noble didn't fare as well in the second round, where he was eliminated by Basque surfer Eneko Acero and Australia's Adam Robertson (who won the Classic in 2008), but he'd already made his point: Scotland doesn't just have world-class waves; it has world-class surfers too. Classic director Matt Wilson emphasises how difficult it is for a surfer like Noble, with a full-time job in the real world, to compete against the pros. 'These guys are surfing heats all day, every day, so for someone like Chris, who works offshore and surfs when he can, to come here and beat them – it's just incredible.'

Traditionally, the winner of the amateur Scottish Surfing Championships, held in March or early April, is granted a wild-card entry into the first round of the Classic. This year, however, due to last-minute no-shows, Wilson was able to hand first-round berths to all four finalists from that event: Mark Cameron, who placed first, Noble, who came second, and also George Watt and Mark Boyd.

After winning the Scottish in previous years, Noble says he had felt the pressure of being the only Scot competing in the Classic; this time, though, he was able to sneak in under the radar. 'Because I'd only entered at the last minute my name wasn't on any of the sheets – nobody asked to speak to me beforehand so I could just go surfing.' Things were very different when the heat was over, however, and Noble was mobbed by friends, well-wishers and journalists. Noble is now 35, so when he talks about Scotland producing its first pro surfer, he isn't talking about himself – he's looking a few years further down the line. A good first step on the road, he believes, would be for Scotland to be recognised as a member nation of the International Surfing Association (ISA). It's a move that would allow Scottish surfers to compete at the annual ISA World Surfing Games, gaining invaluable contest experience, and in his role as president of the Scottish Surfing Federation (SSF) he is working hard to make that happen. 'We're just getting the paperwork together to become recognised and then we're going to join,' he says. 'Right now we're not in a position to put forward a team [for the games] – we don't have enough kids and we don't have the infrastructure. But who's to say in a few years time we're not going to have the ability to push forward?'

End of an era as O'Neill pulls the plug on Thurso's Coldwater Classic

JUST when the Coldwater Classic at Thurso was starting to feel like a regular fixture in the Scottish surfing calendar, the sponsors,

O'Neill, pulled the plug. When I spoke to 2012 Scottish Champ Mark Cameron about it in April of that year, it seemed as if it might only be a temporary hiatus, as the reason O'Neill had given for pulling out was to allow them to focus on a one-off 60th anniversary event in their hometown of Santa Cruz, California. By the autumn, however, when I interviewed O'Neill's European marketing manager Daan Meijer, it was clear that they had no intention of coming back any time soon. Still, for five glorious years, some of the best surfers in the world had competed in Scottish waves – and Scotland's best surfers had shown that they could go toe-to-toe with the pros.

22 April 2012

'It was just so windy, man. The windchill factor was incredible.' Fraserburgh surfer Mark 'Scratch' Cameron is recalling the less-than-perfect conditions that graced this year's Scottish Surfing Championships at Thurso: lumpy 3–5ft waves harried by an icy north-westerly knifing in off the Pentland Firth. At 34 years old, Cameron is getting on a bit in surfing terms, but he's still able to beat young whippersnappers ten years his junior, and this year he picked up his sixth Scottish Championship title, putting him within touching distance of his friend Iain Masson's all-time record of seven. 'It was really blowing onshore so it was taking five or six minutes to paddle out the back,' Cameron says. 'That only gave you time to get two, maybe three waves in a heat, so you had to make sure they were good ones.'

At almost any other surf spot in the country, a howling onshore wind means it's time to go to the pub, but Thurso East, the reef just below Thurso Castle, is special. The shape of the reef, and the angle at which it meets oncoming lines of swell, means that even when it's blowing a hoolie the waves always have some shape, peeling for a good distance before finally exploding onto barnacle-encrusted rocks. In the final, Cameron was run knuckle-chewingly close by Thurso local Chris Noble, who impressed the judges with some powerful turns, but in the end he hung on to win by a fraction of a point. 'Me and Chris have pretty much slugged it out for the last 10 years,' Cameron says of their ongoing rivalry. 'I think there was about half a point in it this time – it was absolutely touch and go.'

Until recently, winning the Scottish Championships would have meant an automatic wildcard entry into round one of the O'Neill Coldwater Classic, formerly the Highland Open – a professional surfing contest that started coming to Thurso in 2006. This year, however, the Classic has been cancelled to allow the sponsors to focus on an event in their hometown of Santa Cruz, California. Cameron says Thurso will feel the effects. 'When the contest comes to town every hotel's booked out, every pub's full for the week, the place is just bustling, but now we've got nothing happening at all. But I'm very, very confident that there'll be more pro contests there again. Most really good waves on the planet are policed by locals who want the waves to themselves, but Thurso is unique – it's such a good wave and the locals are pretty welcoming.'

2014: The year Scotland's surfers won their independence

FOR Scotland to be recognised as an independent surfing nation ahead of the 2014 World Surfing Games in Peru was a major milestone, and for the news to land shortly after that year's

Scottish Independence Referendum gave it an added poignancy. No doubt the more established surfing nations would have been expecting Team Scotland to show up, smile sweetly, wave a few Saltires and finish flat last, but that's not how things panned out – they came a very respectable 16th of 22 countries – not least because the burly reef waves at the contest site at Punta Rocas bore more than a passing resemblance to those at a certain Scottish reef break. . .

24 October 2014

This weekend the best surfers in Scotland will compete as an independent nation at the 50th Anniversary World Surfing Games at Punta Rocas, Peru. The Scottish team were invited to take part last month by the International Surfing Association (ISA). After a review Scotland's application for 'associate membership' – a nation or other organisation not recognised by the International Olympic Committee – was accepted. 'It's the biggest thing that's happened to Scottish surfing in 40 years,' says William Watson, president of the Scottish Surfing Federation (SSF), the governing body that runs surfing north of the Border. 'This has been four years in the making, and Mark Boyd [the SSF's Head of Coaching and Team Management] has been pivotal in making it happen.'

One of the keys to Boyd's case has been that if Hawaii and Wales both have ISA-recognised surf teams, it's only fair that Scotland should have one as well. The names on the team sheet are Mark Cameron and Iain Masson (both Fraserburgh), Andrew Robertson (St Andrews), Mark Boyd (Thurso), Phoebe Strachan (Edinburgh) and Jennifer Wood (Elgin) – and, win or lose, they are in for an unforgettable experience.

Located 45km south of Lima in the district of Punta Negra, Punta Rocas is one of the most popular and consistent point breaks in Peru. The Stormrider Guide (a respected authority on the world's best surf spots) calls it 'regular like clockwork' and it can hold powerful, hollow waves of up to 15 feet over a rocky reef – not too dissimilar, in fact, to Thurso East, Scotland's premier surf spot and a place with which the Scottish team members will be very familiar as it's traditionally where the Scottish National Surfing Championships are held each spring.

But while the waves at Punta Rocas might provide an echo of home, Peruvian surf culture is unique. Wave-riding only really took off in Scotland in the 1960s, but in Peru they've been at it for 3,000 years, initially using 'Totora reed horses' – canoes built out of reeds which were used as fishing boats and then 'surfed' back to shore. Peru also has a proud history of competitive surfing: in 1965 Felipe Pomar won an unexpected World Championship title in big surf at Punta Rocas, ahead of such legendary names as Australia's Nat Young, Hawaii's Fred Hemmings and California's Mike Doyle. More recently, in 2004, Sofia Mulanovic became the first Peruvian to win the Association of Surfing Professionals (ASP) Women's World Tour.

From the ISA's point of view, turning Scotland into a surfing nation in its own right makes a lot of sense. One of the ISA's stated goals is to increase its current membership from 86 to 100 during 2015, as part of a strategy to demonstrate the sport's universal appeal with an eye to future inclusion in the Olympic Programme, so Scotland's case to become number 87 couldn't have been made at a better time. Could we see a Scottish surf team competing at the Olympics one day? In turbulent times like these, it would be unwise to rule anything out.

Emergent islanders: Tiree youngsters
win heats, blow minds

BY THE time I came to do my first official (albeit brief) inter-view with Ben Larg, I'd been visiting Tiree on and off for over a decade, and had come to know his parents Marti and Iona well. The first time I ever saw Ben surf was on an idyllic afternoon at Balephuil, on the south of the island. It was a rare, windless day, on this windiest of islands, low tide, hot sun, turquoise water, waves small but perfectly-formed. As I was coming in from a surf, Marti was ferrying a very young Ben – perhaps only them aged four or five – out into the waves on his longboard. I stopped in the shallows for a while and watched Marti push Ben into a couple of perfect little peelers, and I said something like 'Y'know, if he grows up here and goes surfing whenever there are waves, he's going to be pretty good by the time he's 18.' As it turned out, it didn't take him anywhere near that long.

23 April 2016

Back in October 2005, I interviewed a somewhat exasperated Andy Groom, then head honcho of the Tiree Wave Classic windsurfing contest, about the state of junior watersports on the island. In spite of being one of the most idyllic surfing and windsurfing locations anywhere in the British Isles, Groom felt that Tiree's potential as a training ground for future champions was nowhere near being realised. 'We're trying desperately to get more of the local kids involved,' he told me, 'but they have an inbuilt fear of water. There's no swimming pool on Tiree, their parents don't swim and they don't take them down to the beach. The guys who windsurf here [in the Wave Classic] should be getting their arses kicked by [local] 12-year-old rippers, but they're not.'

The windsurfing scene on the island is certainly looking a lot healthier now than it did then, thanks largely to the efforts of local windsurfer Willy Angus Maclean, who owns the island's Wild Diamond watersports school and has also taken over the running of the Wave Classic from Groom. In recent months, however, it's the island's junior surf scene rather than its junior windsurfing scene that has been making people sit up and take notice. Last October, at the annual Gathering of the Clans surf contest at Thurso, in which teams of surfers from all over the country compete in various different disciplines and age categories, the star of the show was a young surfer from Tiree called Ben Larg. Aged just 10, he pulled off the incredible feat of a second place finish in the under-18s category. (The first place finisher, 17-year-old Andrew Robertson, had previously represented Scotland at international level, so there was hardly any shame in losing to him.) This wasn't just a flash in the pan either – at the Scottish Surfing Championships at Thurso earlier this month, Larg and fellow Tiree surfer Finn MacDonald dominated the junior divisions, MacDonald winning the under-18s category and Larg (now a veteran at age 11) winning the under-14s. For MacDonald, 15, it was a remarkable result given that this was the first time he'd ever surfed at Thurso, and Larg surfed so well that Andy Bennetts, one of the first people ever to surf in Scotland back in the mid-1960s, described him as 'an amazing talent with a bright future' – praise indeed from someone who, when it comes to Scottish surfing, has literally seen it all.

A few days after the contest, I catch up with Larg and MacDonald, both of them obviously still buzzing from their big wins. 'It was a wee bit windy,' says Larg of the final day of the contest, which saw howling offshore winds, 'and it was quite big as well, maybe about five-foot. In the final it died down a wee bit, but it still wasn't an easy wave.' MacDonald says he took a while to adapt to surfing a new spot: 'In the first couple of heats I didn't think I'd done very well, but by the finals I was doing a wee bit better – I was getting to know the break a bit better. In the final there was one really good wave – I got a nice long ride and did a few turns on it.'

Surf instructor Craig 'Suds' Sutherland helps run the Tiree Surf Club during the summer. 'Finn and Ben have been surfing on Tiree for so long now I think it would have been an upset for them not to have done well,' he laughs. 'They started at a young age and they're pretty much in the water the whole time. They're in the water for six hours a day easy in the summertime when it's good. I think there will be loads more [good young surfers from Tiree] after these guys too,' he adds. 'On the club days we'll maybe get about 15 in the water and they get good so fast it's just ridiculous. Initially it was just Ben and Finn and then a few more kids started coming and then all of a sudden the interest started spiking. If I'm doing lessons in the summer, those guys will be out the back absolutely tearing it up and you can tell that all the kids in the lessons are looking at them and just want to emulate them.'

Following their wins at the Scottish Championships, it came as a surprise to precisely no-one to find that the Scottish Surfing Federation had selected both Larg and MacDonald to represent Scotland at the ISA World Junior Surfing Championships in the Azores in September and at the European Juniors in Morocco in December.

Mark Boyd's back-up board drama at UK Pro

THIS UK Pro Surf Tour result for Mark Boyd was something of a changing of the guard moment for Scottish surfing. Since the turn of the millennium, only two Scottish surfers had ever been crowned Scottish champion up to this point: Chris Noble and Mark Cameron. While it would take Boyd another couple of years to finally win the Nationals (George Watt of Fraserburgh actually broke the Noble-Cameron stranglehold in 2017) this strong showing against the best surfers in the UK was a major statement. Boyd may not have been quite as effortless in the tube as Noble or as lightning quick on his feet as Cameron. What he had (and still has) that the other two lacked, however, was a full-blooded power-surfing act that felt like a glorious throwback to the days of Aussie pros Tom Carroll and Gary Elkerton. Not many surfers can be said to manhandle the waves at Thurso East – usually it's more a case of polite negotiation, harnessing the wave's energy rather than pushing against it. When Boyd throws his considerable frame into a turn, though, you almost feel sorry for the wave.

12 November 2016

Of all the Scottish surfers given wildcard entries to the UK Pro Surf Tour event at Thurso at the end of last month, Mark Boyd was perhaps the least well-prepared. 'I've been working non-stop through the summer and autumn and just managed to get the time off for the contest,' he says. 'Actually it felt like I was trying to re-learn how to surf wave by wave during the comp, which isn't ideal going up against guys who have been surfing and competing all summer.'

In spite of his lack of match fitness, however, Boyd progressed to the final, where he finished fourth behind some of the top pros in the land – Reubyn Ash (ranked 2nd), Jobe Harriss (ranked 1st) and Jayce Robinson (ranked 12th). Even if he'd been camped out in front of the reef at Thurso East for the previous six months, surfing it every time it got good, making the final would still have been a huge achievement; coming off the back of a prolonged surf break, though – particularly given how quickly surfing fitness can fade – it's a wonder he made it past the first round.

That said, Boyd did have a couple of important factors in his favour. For a start, he has clocked up enough surfing time at Thurso East over the years to be able to feel at home amongst its heaving grey walls. Plus, conditions on Day One were well-suited to his large frame and powerful surfing style – double overhead waves made choppy and unpredictable by a stiff westerly breeze. 'A lot of the guys were struggling a bit with these conditions,' he says, 'but I felt really comfortable as we surf in these type of conditions often. I also wonder if this is perhaps one of the rare occasions where being a taller, heavier surfer may actually help – negotiating chop!'

Boyd didn't exactly have an easy draw in the first round, finding himself up against current British champ and ratings leader Jobe Harriss of England. However, he had a plan and he stuck to it: 'I picked the right waves, built on each score and finished my last wave with a big turn which got me a good score,' he says. 'In those conditions that was enough to place first in that heat quite convincingly, which I was pleased with, as I did see Jobe get a barrel and do a couple of turns too. It felt good, and gave me a bit of confidence to start off the event.'

By the second day of the waiting period the wind had made Thurso East all-but unsurfable, so the contest caravan decamped to the reef at Sandside, 12 miles to the west, where the junior heats were held in head-high left-handers fanned by a cross-off-shore wind.

In the boys' under-16s category, 11-year-old Ben Larg of Tiree surfed strongly and was unlucky not to make it past the first round. His compatriot Andrew Robertson of St Andrews, however, bade farewell to the junior divisions in fine style. He stormed all the way into the under-18s final before the contest was called off for the day due to the low tide exposing the reef. Then, back at pumping Thurso East the following morning, he placed third in the final, in what will be his last competition before moving up to the men's division.

Speaking of which, the men's division quarter finals back at Thurso almost saw Boyd eliminated. First he was involved in an altercation with fellow Scot Chris Clarke about wave priority (they made up in the car park afterwards), then his leash snapped, forcing him to swim to shore and pick up a back-up board. With just eight minutes on the clock, he finally made it back to the line-up but with no scores on the board to speak of things didn't look good. 'I was absolutely exhausted,' he says. 'But it kind of relaxed me, knowing that the odds were stacked against me. I picked off a wave straight away and managed a combination of pretty average turns but it got me back in the game and into second place [first and second place go through to the next round]. Then I got another backup score which maintained my second position until the end of the heat.'

In Boyd's semi-final, the lead see-sawed between Boyd and England's Liam Turner until Harriss snagged a late barrel, catapulting himself into the lead, with Boyd in second also going through. In the final, things didn't really come together – 'I was really disappointed with myself,' says Boyd – but given all the drama earlier in the day, not to mention his lack of training, it was a minor miracle he was there at all. 'I really want to try and eliminate that kind of inconsistency from my surfing,' he adds. If he manages that, he could be the man to beat at Thurso for years to come.

Camels and Anchors: A Moroccan adventure for Scotland's junior surfers

WHEN William Watson and Mark Boyd were battling through piles of admin to get Scotland recognised as a surfing nation in its own right, this is surely the kind of thing they had in mind: Scotland's best young surfers travelling to Morocco to compete in the Eurosurf Junior Games – a trip that also saw them getting to ride camels and surf the legendary, reeling rights of Anchor Point into the bargain.

6 January 2017

It's been quite a year for Scotland's junior surf team, particularly when you consider that they've only been able to compete on the world stage since 2014. With such limited experience you might reasonably expect them to be propping up the international standings for a few more years yet while they find their feet, but in September they held their own at the World Junior Surfing Championships in the Azores, finishing a respectable 27th out of 38 competing countries, and this month, at the Eurosurf Junior Games in Agadir, Morocco, they defied expectations again, finishing ninth out of 16 teams taking part. More importantly, they seem to be having fun – in Agadir they also picked up the award for the competition's friendliest team.

Team manager Marti Larg, who runs Blackhouse Watersports on the Isle of Tiree, describes the Moroccan result as 'fantastic' and it's hard to disagree. If you'd told William Watson and Mark Boyd of the Scottish Surfing Federation back in 2014, as they waded through seemingly endless piles of paperwork to get Scotland officially recognised by the International Surfing Association (ISA), that in only a couple of years' time the Scottish junior team would be doing this well, they would have been delighted.

A key part of Team Scotland's success in Agadir was a strong showing from the multi-tasking Andrew Robertson from St Andrews, who finished seventh in the under-18s longboard category, 11th in the under-18 bodyboard and 15th in the under-18s shortboard; his longboard result was all the more remarkable when you consider the somewhat old school tanker he was riding, as Larg explains. 'He hired a longboard [for the contest] and you should've seen this thing – it was 10 foot long and it was the last one in the shop. It was so heavy he pretty much needed the whole team to carry it to the beach. He was surfing it in double-overhead conditions, too – the boy deserves a medal.'

Conditions at Agadir's exposed beachbreak were tricky to begin with, but they improved as the competition wore on. 'The first couple of days it'd been raining a lot, so you had all this river water rushing out to sea,' says Larg. 'The sea was quite turbulent and the swell was big, so the conditions were rough at the start, but then it stopped raining, and the sea went from being chocolate brown to a normal colour and the waves just got better and better. There was still a really strong current, though, sweeping you from right to left across the bay, so you would have to paddle out in the middle [of the break] then drift out to the left and paddle round the back.'

Although Robertson led the charge, it was a strong team performance overall: of the shortboarders, Clover Christopherson finished 19th in the under-18 girls, with Iona McLachlan 21st; Finn MacDonald finished 21st in both the under-16 and under-18 boys and 11-year-old Ben Larg, hero of the Azores campaign and competing here in spite of a spot of Agadir belly, still managed 19th in the under-14 boys. In the bodyboard categories, Oisin Strachan placed 19th overall in the boys under-18s, with Mickey Wimbledon in 11th in the under-16s, while Christopherson came 9th in the girls under-18s and 19th in the under-16s – particularly impressive given that she was also unwell.

Of course, results are by no means the be-all and end-all at an event like this – Morocco is an incredible place for a young surfer to visit, and the members of Team Scotland took full advantage, from sampling the local cuisine to taking camel rides on the beach. There was even a visit to Anchor Point – a legendary right-hander that is on every serious surfer's bucket list. The crew found it in prime condition, too, and – judging by the pictures – caught their fair share of good waves.

The contest site itself, Larg says, was 'a bit intimidating' and had an industrial feel, with an oil refinery and canneries for mackerel, tuna and sardines nearby. The people, though, he describes as 'the warmest folk you've ever met' and there is now talk of setting up a regular, informal competition between the Scottish surf team and the local Anza Surf Club. Training sessions in the reeling pointbreaks of Morocco each winter would certainly do Scotland's surfers no end of good, and it would also be interesting to see what the Moroccans make of Scotland. As a man in a hat once said, this could be the beginning of a beautiful friendship . . .

Megan Mackay makes history in Norway

FROM the sweltering heat of Morocco to a snowy Norwegian beach, by 2017 Scotland's top surfers were gaining valuable competitive experience wherever they could find it. Megan Mackay's remarkable first place finish at the Nordic Surf Games was a real landmark: the first time a Scottish surfer had ever won an international event.

11 April 2017

On a bright, chilly morning in April 2010, I found myself in the farmyard overlooking the reef at Thurso East, sitting in a van belonging to many-times Scottish surfing champion Chris Noble while he munched on a bacon and egg roll and considered the future of Scottish surfing. 'At the end of the day we've got waves that are just as good as anywhere, and we can surf just as good as these guys,' he said, motioning in the direction of the water, where some of the best pro surfers in the world were contesting that year's O'Neill Coldwater Classic. It wasn't just empty talk: Noble had proven his point the day before by becoming the first Scot to progress from the opening round of the Classic since its inception in 2006. But when he looked into the future, the 35 year-old wasn't dreaming big dreams for his own career, but imagining what the next generation might achieve.

'We're just getting the paperwork together to become recognised [by the International Surfing Association],' he told me – he was president of the Scottish Surfing Federation at the time – 'and then we're going to join. Right now we're not in a position to put forward a team – we don't have enough kids and we don't have the infrastructure. But who's to say that in a few years' time we're not going to have the ability to push forward?'

Fast forward to the present day, and Scotland is indeed a member of the ISA, and has been sending teams to ISA-sanctioned contests all over the world since 2014, exceeding expectations at almost every turn. And earlier this year, at the Nordic Surf Games in Jæren, Norway, another milestone was reached when 19-year-old Megan Mackay from Macduff became the first Scottish surfer ever to win an international competition. 'I couldn't believe it,' she says down the line from the University of Aberdeen, where she's studying Geology. 'The waves were kind of similar to home. I found the water a bit warmer than here, but I found the air temperature much colder – I remember just shivering whenever I came out of the water. It was snowing one day too, but it was really cool – like something in a film.'

Held at the end of February, the Nordic Surf Games were open to surfers of all nationalities but mostly saw competitors from Norway, Sweden and Denmark, with a few more exotic countries such as Brazil and Hawaii also represented. The Scottish Surfing Federation fielded a team of four: Mackay (women's open), Jamie Marshall (longboard), Mark Boyd (men's open) and Elliot Young (Juniors). Like most surf contests, the Nordic Games have a knock-out format, with four surfers in each heat and the top two finishers progressing to the next round. 'In my first heat the conditions were really good,' says Mackay, 'head high waves, offshore wind and the waves really had a bit of punch to them. I came second in that heat – I got a couple of good left-handers and a couple of good rights as well. Then I came second again in round two. Again I got a couple of good waves but I missed out on first place because I didn't complete one of my turns properly. I was a bit annoyed about that, but I learned from each experience and built on that in the other heats.'

By the time the semi-finals rolled around, the waves had lost a bit of power, so Mackay made the decision to switch boards:

'The next day it had dropped off quite a lot and the wind had turned onshore so I took out a different board. It's one I use for Aberdeen when it gets . . . well . . . crap! It's a Rusty Dwart and it's just better for messier, sloppy conditions – it just felt right under my feet.'

It turned out to be an inspired decision: Mackay came first in her semi-final heat, and was on song when she reached the final. 'My first wave in the final was a left-hand wave. I took off, completed a big top turn, did a big bottom turn and then it walled up on the inside and I managed to complete another turn. I remember hearing everybody cheering. Then another left-hander came through and I managed to complete a few good turns on that.' Mackay didn't know what position she was in until the last few minutes of the heat, when the commentator read out the scores over the loudspeaker and she realised she was in first. 'I was really hoping that no more waves would come through, but then Guro [Aanestad of Norway, the reigning champion] got a really good wave and I thought ach dammit, I think that's me lost my position. But I think my manoeuvres were in a more critical part of the wave, so in the end I got the higher scores. It was really good to see girls from other coldwater countries – how good they were, and how we've all got to go through the same struggle through the cold to get good waves.'

When Team Scotland brought claymores to a fencing match

THERE'S an art to surfing small, fickle beachbreak waves. With world-class reef breaks like Thurso East on their doorstep, however, you could forgive Scotland's elite surfers for spending more of their free time rocketing through heaving 10 foot barrels than honing their chop-hops in two-foot close-outs. One side effect of this is that their competition results in smaller waves, such as those that greeted the 2017 World Surfing Games in Biarritz, have tended to disappoint. Never mind – at least there was some fun to be had with the live commentary. . .

3 June 2017

'And zat is our surfeur from Scotland . . . Mark Cameron . . . 39 years of age from Frazzer-bruh . . . from Frazzer-burrr . . .' One of the highlights of watching Team Scotland compete in the ISA World Surfing Games in Biarritz last week was listening to the multi-national team of announcers on the live webcast mangling Scottish place names. Sadly we didn't have anyone from Kirkcudbright or Ecclefechan or even Milngavie taking part, but the home town of the 2016 Scottish champion caused more than enough commentary box consternation all by itself.

Cameron was giving his opponents a tricky time out in the water, too. Five minutes into his 20-minute Round One heat he was sitting pretty in second place, behind Cristian Portelli of Sweden but ahead of the hotly tipped José Ferreira of Portugal, with the top two finishers advancing to Round Two and the surfer in third having to do battle in the last chance saloon of the repechage. Over the next 10 minutes, however, the heat started to slip away: Ferreira posted a couple of solid scores to leapfrog into first place while Portelli drew further ahead. But then, with three minutes remaining, Cameron paddled into one of the better waves of the day and, for a few moments at least, it looked as if we might be in for a last-ditch upset.

After hopping nimbly to his feet, he flowed through a fast

bottom turn, cranked a sweeping gouge off the top and then raced through a frothy inside section before bouncing off the lip one more time as the wave exploded onto the sand. The noises coming from the commentary box were encouraging – 'nice first turn,' 'Yeah, right off the lip with flow, with speed' – but when the judges eventually delivered their verdict the score wasn't quite high enough to carry him through.

Cameron's repechage heat the following day was held in small, inconsistent surf, and he was beaten into fourth place by Adi Gluska of Israel, Logan Landry of Canada and Jhonny Alfonso of Panama. The rest of Team Scotland didn't fare much better: Scott Main and Chris Clarke were also eliminated at the repechage stage while Mark Boyd, after progressing convincingly from his repechage heat, was eliminated in Round Two. With both the women's surfers, Shoana Blackadder and Jen Wood, also going out in the repechage, Team Scotland ended up ranked 38th out of 47 competing nations. Of all the nations that entered a full complement of four men and two women, only China finished with a lower points tally.

That said, from a Scottish perspective the conditions in Biarritz could hardly have been worse, particularly for the men, who at times had to compete in waves that were almost comically small. Cameron, Main, Clarke and Boyd are at their best when surfing thundering ten-foot barrels at Thurso East, so the sleepy two-foot beachbreak waves on offer in Biarritz were never going to allow them to play to their strengths. More than once, they looked like men accustomed to fighting with claymores who had been invited to try their hand at a spot of fencing.

One of the rewards for contributing to the Crowdfunder to help cover Team Scotland's costs in Biarritz was a film called 01847 by Thurso lensman Malcolm Anderson, and it shows what these surfers can do when the waves get serious. They may not be the best in the world at generating momentum in knee-high dribble, but when it comes to dealing with the raw power of the North Atlantic in the middle of the winter storm season, you get the feeling they could probably give most people a run for their money.

For the time being, then, Team Scotland's success on the world stage will probably have a lot to do with where competitions are held: the bigger the waves, the better they'll do. In the longer term, however, it's interesting to speculate about how Wavegarden Scotland, the proposed artificial wave pool at Ratho, near Edinburgh, might affect our surfers' chances in more modest conditions. The so-called 'Cove' technology the Wavegarden team is planning to install would allow waves of various shapes and sizes to be served up to order. As Boyd puts it: 'A facility like [this] would give the Scottish surfing team a huge edge, helping us prepare for different conditions.' Wavegarden Scotland submitted their planning application this week, so who knows? The 2027 Scottish champ might just come from easy-to-pronounce Ratho.

Surfers on the golf course: an unlikely venue for the Scottish Nationals

IT WAS a long time coming, but after several years of near misses Mark Boyd finally bagged his first Scottish Nationals win in April 2018. Sure, the contest took place in less-than-perfect conditions at Sinclair's Bay, beside Wick Golf Club, as opposed to in flawless barrels at his favoured Thurso East, but he didn't seem to mind. The jinx was lifted, and he finally had his hands on the storied old trophy. Even as Boyd was celebrating his title, however, the next generation were gearing up to challenge him for it. Note the fleeting reference here to young Craig McLachlan, winner of both the U14 and U18 boys titles – we'll be hearing more from him soon.

26 April 2018

Any golfers planning to squeeze in 18 holes at Wick Golf Club on Easter Saturday would have been surprised to find the car park teeming with wetsuit-clad surfers. Traditionally the annual Scottish Surfing Championships are held at the better-known spots along the north coast of Caithness – usually either Thurso East or Brims Ness – but when this year's contest began, on 31 March, the best conditions in the area were to be found on the east coast, at Sinclair's Bay, so that's where the majority of the event took place.

'Wick Golf Club were very kind and allowed competitors and spectators to use their toilets and changing rooms,' says eventual Men's Open winner Mark Boyd. 'Sinclair's Bay is a fantastic contest site. I've surfed over there a lot – it's kind of the forgotten coast in Caithness with the north coast being so famous, so it was pretty cool having an event there.'

Boyd, 31, is based in Thurso and has long been one of Scotland's best competitive surfers, finishing runner-up in the Men's Open division of the Scottish Championships in 2016 and 2017 and regularly making the top three since 2009. 'It feels great to finally get my name on the trophy after coming so close so many times,' he says. 'I definitely feel like I've got the monkey off my back.' Boyd also ended Fraserburgh's long-standing domination of the Men's Open category – before he broke his own personal hoodoo the title had been won by a Broch surfer every year since 1995. In a nod to the past, this year the trophies were awarded by three of Scotland's great surfing pioneers of the 1960s and 70s: Bill Batten, Ian Wishart and Andy Bennetts. 'It was an honour to receive the trophy from Bill himself,' says Boyd, 'the first ever Scottish national surfing champion.'

The majority of the contest took place over the weekend at Sinclair's Bay with the bodyboard, longboard and junior divisions all decided in sunny waist to chest-high waves. Young Michael Wimbledon-Hall from Dunbar, identified as one to watch in this column not so long ago, took out both the Junior and Senior Bodyboard titles while Chris Clarke won the longboard title. Clover Christopherson won the Under-18 Girls, while in the boys' divisions Craig McLachlan won the Under-14s and Under-18s and Ben Larg won the Under-16s – both of those surfers are still just 12, and look set to dominate the junior divisions for years to come.

On Monday there was enough swell coming through to make Thurso East contestable, so the event moved back to its spiritual home for the final rounds of the Men's and Women's Open divisions and also the Masters final. In the latter category, Craig 'Suds' Sutherland faced a seemingly impossible task, with a final that also featured two multiple Men's Open winners: Mark Cameron and Chris Noble. Cameron held the lead until late on, when Sutherland found a rare fast left-hander and put in a stylish ride to take top spot. This was Sutherland's first Masters title – and there was another maiden victory for Phoebe Strachan who beat Shoana Blackadder into second place to win the Women's Open, after finishing runner-up in 2017.

In the final of the Men's Open, Boyd found himself up against Sutherland, Andrew MacLeod and last year's winner George

Watt. 'Georgie got off to a decent start with a good score that really put the pressure on,' says Boyd. 'In the past I may have let that affect me and I'd have lost my cool a bit but I stayed confident right through.' Going into the last five minutes of the heat, Boyd found himself with a marginal lead and first priority (that is, as the surfer with first refusal on any good waves that come through.)I knew all I had to do at this point was choose a good wave, not only to improve my lead but also to keep my competitors from getting it,' he says. There was a bit of a lull and then a set finally came – the pressure was really on at this point for me to make the right decisions. I looked at the first one but didn't paddle for it, maintaining my priority. Then the second one came – it was a good wave with good shape and I knew this was the one but my friend Andrew MacLeod got a bit confused with the priority situation and also took off on that wave which meant I couldn't surf it. This was a worrying time for me, because I didn't know if Georgie had done anything to increase his lead in those dying minutes, but fortunately the situation didn't change. I was a bit frustrated not to get the opportunity to really hit the lip like I wanted to and win more convincingly but I'm delighted to be the 2018 Scottish National Champion.'

How Team Scotland got tangled in Olympic red tape

THE IOC's decision to make surfing an official Olympic sport was celebrated by wave-riders across the world, but it had unfortunate consequences for Scotland's hard-won standing as an officially recognised surfing nation. All that paperwork over all those years and then this. . .

27 September 2018

In October 2014, in the aftermath of the Scottish Independence Referendum, it was a pleasure to be able to report that Scotland's surfers, at least, would soon be celebrating their independence, having won permission to send a national team to the World Surfing Games at Punta Rocas, Peru. It was, the president of the Scottish Surfing Federation (SSF) William Watson told me at the time, 'the biggest thing that's happened to Scottish surfing in 40 years.'

At this stage the SSF's application for recognition by the International Surfing Association (ISA) was still under review, but while the paperwork was being sorted out, they had been invited to field a team as a gesture of encouragement and goodwill. Scotland's surfers didn't exactly sweep all before them at the 50th edition of the Games, but they still achieved a very respectable 16th place finish, just ahead of wave-rich Tahiti. Any sense that a Scottish surf team was some sort of chuckle-worthy novelty act was instantly dispelled at that first event.

The following year, after yet more paperwork, Scotland finally gained recognition as an 'associate member' of the ISA – that is, as a nation recognised by the ISA but not by the International Olympic Committee (IOC) – and the team went on to compete in the World Surfing Games in Nicaragua in 2015, Costa Rica in 2016, and France in 2017. I was looking forward to following their exploits at the World Surfing Games in Tahara, Japan this year too, but was surprised to discover that there would be no Scottish team at the event. So I called Mark Boyd, secretary of the SSF and also captain of the Scottish team, and asked him what was going on. Turns out that the inclusion of surfing in the 2020 Olympics, while an exciting prospect for the sport as a whole, is a bit of a nightmare for Team Scotland, who, having only recently gained their independence as a surfing nation now seem to be on the verge of losing it again.

'It's very complicated,' says Boyd, and he isn't kidding. Because the 2019 and 2020 editions of the World Surfing Games will be used to decide which nations qualify for the 2020 Olympics, only national teams recognised by the IOC are able to take part in those two events. Initially, then, it looked as if Scotland and other associate members of the ISA like Hawaii and the Channel Islands would only be able to compete in two World Surfing Games every four years. However, the news then got even worse, as Boyd explains:

'The Olympic qualification cycle is only two years, but American teams qualify through the World Surfing Games for the Pan American Games, which is their qualification opportunity for the Olympics. Basically [the ISA] didn't want Hawaii competing as well as the USA [at the 2018 World Surfing Games] so they just put a blanket ban on all the non-National Olympic Committee countries including Tahiti, the Channel Islands, Scotland, England, Wales . . . I did ask if we'd be able to compete in the years outwith the cycle and they said in theory yes, but that wasn't a definite answer. We're still hoping there's going to be one year out of every four we're going to be able to go [to the World Surfing Games] but we'll see.'

There has been a British team competing at this week's World Surfing Games in Japan, but there's no Scottish interest – it's made up of five English surfers and one Welshman, with the selections having been made based on previous results. And as Boyd points out, the new set-up doesn't just hurt Scottish surfing by giving its top athletes fewer opportunities to compete at the highest level. 'This is also a pretty negative thing for us as far as funding's concerned,' he says. 'There are opportunities for more funding from Sport Scotland if you perform at world championship level, but they've taken that away. And not only that – UK Sport have confirmed that they won't be funding any new sports, so surfing isn't going to be getting any funding [from there either].

'Nothing really positive has come out of this thus far,' Boyd concludes, 'but we wish the team that's over there all the best and hope that maybe there's a chance of a British team getting into the Olympics. All our focus now is on trying to get a Scottish athlete into the team before then. The British Surfing Championships will be at Thurso in 2020, and that will be within the Olympic qualification cycle, so we're hoping that a bit of a home advantage might help some of our surfers get into the British team. That'd be fantastic, so that's what we're setting our sights on now.'

Best of rivals: celebrating the Boyd-McLachlan axis

WITH Chris Noble and Mark Cameron finally starting to relax their decade-long grip on the Scottish Nationals trophy as they moved further into middle-age, Mark Boyd might have been forgiven for thinking that, after taking his first, long-awaited title in 2018, he could at last look forward to a few years of dominance. Young Thurso surfer Craig McLachlan had other ideas, however, and by 2023 the Cameron-Noble rivalry at the pinnacle of Scottish surfing had been replaced by a Boyd-McLachlan axis. Boyd won in 2018, 2019 and 2022 but McLachlan triumphed in 2021 and 2023, and he would take home the trophy again in 2024. McLachlan's 2023 win was perhaps his most impressive, however (at least, at time of writing). Brims Ness at size isn't a place to toy with but McLachlan didn't look like he was merely surviving out there – he looked like he was having fun.

20 May 2023

Last month, something remarkable happened at the Scottish National Surfing Championships at Brims Ness – an experts-only surf spot a few miles to the west of Thurso, where the full force of the Atlantic Ocean comes into explosive contact with a series of shallow rock slabs. Not only did 17-year-old local Craig McLachlan win the Junior Boys division – no mean feat in itself – he also surfed his way into the Men's Open final, where he faced previous event winners Mark Boyd and Mark Cameron and another seasoned competitor, Andrew Robertson.

For most 17-year-old surfers, that would have been more than enough of an excuse to crack open a celebratory (non-alcoholic) beer and relax, but McLachlan wasn't done yet. In the fiercely-contested four-man heat he surfed out of his skin in fast, hollow, overhead waves. He thwacked his top turns with authority, toyed with the axe-like lip of the Brims breakers as if a beating on the shallow, unforgiving reef wasn't even a remote possibility, and landed high-risk manoeuvres so effortlessly that his knees appeared to be made of the same rubber as his wetsuit. He didn't just win, he won in style, with two eight-point scores (out of a possible ten) putting him comfortably ahead of last year's champ Mark Boyd in second.

'The first day [of the contest] was pretty hard to surf, but by the second day the waves were super fun,' he says over the phone from Tiree, where he's spending some time with celebrated Scottish big wave surfer Ben Larg and his family. 'It felt like I got a pretty nice rhythm going through the comp on the second day, which for me is a really special feeling.'

McLachlan certainly hit the ground running at the start of the second and final day of the Nationals, with a high-speed tube ride and perfectly-timed exit that scored him a near-perfect 9.7. In terms of his compact body positioning on the wave and the way he uncoiled himself to come rocketing out from under its falling lip, it wasn't dissimilar to 2000 world surfing champion Sunny Garcia's memorable second wave at Brims back in April 2008, when he made an unexpected appearance at that year's Highland Open pro contest. Sure, McLachlan's barrel may have been shorter, but his wave was bigger and faster, and the exit – with the wave about to detonate both in front of him and behind him – more critical.

'I watched the heat before mine and nobody was really getting any waves, so I was a little bit nervous,' he says. 'I wasn't sure how it was going to go, but I knew there were good waves out there and I got that one, and that just set me up for the rest of the day.' Incredibly, this is actually McLachlan's second Men's Open title, following his maiden win in 2021, and it means that between them he and Boyd have now won the division five times in the last five years it's been contested. Boyd won his first two titles in 2018 and 2019, the Nationals had to be cancelled due to the pandemic in 2020, and then, following McLachlan's win in 2021, Boyd won again in 2022. To long-time observers, it feels as if a new rivalry may be developing, perhaps similar to the era-defining one between Mark Cameron and Chris Noble that saw Cameron win seven titles to Noble's six between 1999 and 2016.

'Boydie's so switched on technically with his surfing, and so strategic, so it's always super-fun to surf against him,' says McLachlan. 'There's quite a big age gap between us, so when I was younger I used to really look up to him and I still think he surfs incredibly, so I'm always happy to surf a heat against him.' McLachlan is keen to point out that his fellow finalist Andrew Robertson could also feature prominently in future battles for the title of Scotland's best male surfer. 'I surf with Andrew quite a lot,' he says. 'Just this last winter he moved up to Thurso and he has some crazy natural talent so he's progressing at such a fast rate. It's cool to be able to surf with somebody closer to my age because in Thurso there's not really anyone else my age that I get to surf with.'

Born and raised in Thurso, McLachlan first got into surfing via his older sister Iona – interviewed in these pages back in 2019, after she won the Women's Open division at that year's Scottish Nationals. 'My sister sort of surfed a little bit by herself,' he says, 'and then a club started in Thurso and we knew the people that started it. My sister started going for the first year, and in the second year I joined and from then I just couldn't stay out of the water.'

In addition to his two Scottish titles, McLachlan also turned heads by becoming last year's British Junior Champion. The next challenge on his radar is the 2023 Eurosurf contest, staged in Santa Cruz, Portugal from 21–30 July, where he'll be representing Scotland in the men's division alongside Marks Boyd and Cameron. 'It's kinda hard to say what the waves will be like,' he says. 'It could be absolutely huge or it could be tiny.' Whatever the conditions, however, some of Europe's leading surfing nations could be in for a shock if they come up against Team Scotland.

Phoebe Strachan finds order
in Portuguese chaos

JUST paddling a longboard out through the thumping shore-break at the 2023 European Surfing Championships in Portugal was an achievement. Finding a half-decent wave to ride in all the chaos? Even more so. Making the last eight of the competition when you don't even consider yourself a longboarder? Impossible, surely? Phoebe Strachan might not have fared quite so well against Europe's best had the contest been held in perfect, longboard-friendly peelers, but in a turbulent, churning line-up swept by powerful currents, she was able to put some of the grit and determination developed surfing back home to good use.

5 August 2023

There are certain surf spots, and certain kinds of conditions, that are ideally suited to longboarding – that is, surfing on boards nine-feet long and over. Malibu in California is an obvious example, preferably on a windless day, with glassy, waist-high waves peeling all the way along the famous point. Waikiki on the Hawaiian island of Oahu is another, perhaps with its gently surging breakers fanned by a light, fragrant offshore breeze. It's at places like these, where the waves break cleanly and predictably, that longboarders are able to perform their most stylish manoeuvres, cross-stepping to the nose to hang five toes over the end of their board, perhaps even hanging 10, before gliding back to the tail, flowing through a graceful drop-knee cutback and then setting up to do it all over again.

However, there are certain spots and conditions where longboards work less well. All that surface area provides a wonderful, stable platform for performing tricks in small waves, but in bigger, hollower surf, it can become a liability – even paddling out to where the waves are breaking can be a trial. A surfer on a skinny six-foot shortboard can easily duck-dive under a six-foot wave. Sinking nine feet of foam under the water requires considerably more strength and skill, however, and if you don't have enough momentum to duck-dive your only real alternative is the turtle-roll; get that wrong as a big wave approaches and you'll wish you hadn't.

On the whole, conditions for this year's European Surfing Championships (Eurosurf for short) in Santa Cruz, Portugal, were far from longboard-friendly, which makes it even more remarkable that Phoebe Strachan of Thurso advanced all the way to the last eight in the women's longboard category, even posting a win in her three-woman second round repechage heat, knocking the talented Italian surfer Francesca Rubegni out of the competition in the process.

The waves for this round were a solid five-to-six-feet, and backed by a stiff cross-onshore wind that made them break unpredictably. One second, a surfer could be flying along what seemed like an open face, the next they could suddenly be engulfed in an explosion of whitewater. Even paddling out to the take-off spot was a challenge. 'I got absolutely destroyed in the shorebreak to start with,' Strachan says. 'But in the end [the conditions] seemed to actually work quite well in my favour – I just put my head down and paddled.'

Once she'd negotiated the shorebreak, Strachan started the heat strongly, skipping down the face of a big, choppy right-hander and hanging on through a tricky cutback to ride all the way through to the inside. With seven minutes left of the 20-minute heat she managed to cling on through another rodeo-ride of a right, giving her a slender lead over Rubegni and Sofia Soori of Sweden. At this point, however, the strong current running through the competition zone started to play a role, pushing Strachan and Soori out of position. 'They were shouting over the Tannoy that I wasn't even in the comp zone any more because

I'd been washed so far down,' says Strachan, 'so I was having to battle just to get back into the comp zone to be able to catch another wave.'

While Strachan and Soori fought against the current, Rubegni had her pick of the waves. With a minute and a half to go she finally took off on a promising looking left, built up some speed, banked off the top . . . but then lost her balance and fell. 'It will be hard for her to get back to the line-up in the next 55 seconds' predicted one of the commentators, and so it proved, with Strachan hanging on for the win. She may have been beaten in the next round, but by making the last eight Strachan still posted Scotland's best result of this year's Eurosurf, helping the team to 12th place overall – an even more impressive feat when you consider she mostly rides a shortboard. 'I'm not a longboarder,' she says. 'I just took one for the team and entered it because we didn't have anyone else who would.'

Strachan also competed in the women's shortboard, alongside Clover Christopherson and Olivia MacKay, and Team Scotland also fielded surfers in the men's shortboard and men's longboard categories. Mostly they all made early exits, but there were still some memorable moments. 'I really enjoyed seeing Craig [McLachlan] getting through his Round One heat,' says Strachan, 'that was pretty exciting because he beat some pretty good boys. And also seeing Olivia compete – she's one of my groms who I've coached pretty much since she started surfing, and for her to make not only the adult team but also to compete and make it through a round, that was pretty special. I've seen her all the way through, from starting off on a foamie [foam board] to competing on the world stage.'

Next generation longboarding
with Ansel Parkin

SINCE 2005, when the Scottish National Surfing Championships
were revived following a five-year hiatus, they have usually been
held on the north coast, either at Thurso East or Brims Ness.
These locations regularly serve up the fast, hollow waves favoured
by shortboarders, but they are less well-suited to the more sedate
art of longboarding, where elegant drop-knee turns and balletic
cross-stepping to the nose tend to be the aim of the game. This
has often led to longboarding heats being run in the kinds of
conditions where most people wouldn't even dream of paddling
out on a nine-foot log. Good news all round, then, when the
longboarding division of the Nationals moved to the more longboard-friendly waves of Pease Bay in 2024, where young Ansel
Parkin showed that Scotland's next generation of surfers are both
fiercely talented and happy riding anything.

22 May 2024

It's mid-afternoon on Saturday 27 April, and the Scottish
National Longboard Championships are under way at Pease Bay
in the Scottish Borders. The spring sun may be shining down
from an almost cloudless sky, but the icy wind knifing in off
the North Sea is making things feel distinctly wintry. The waves
are small, perhaps only a couple of feet at most, and crumbling
unpredictably thanks to the onshore wind. It's surfable – just –
but these are by no means the conditions the event organisers
would have been hoping for. Still, longboards (boards over nine
feet in length) are designed to work in small surf, and in spite of
the lacklustre waves on offer, 15-year-old Ansel Parkin is turning

his Round One heat in the Men's division into something of a masterclass in how to generate speed from almost nothing. Even from a distance, he's obviously a good bit smaller than the two surfers he's up against, Joe Rodger and Robbie Lawson. But while the other two are understandably struggling to find rideable waves in the blown-out chaos, Parkin seems able to pick up every ripple that comes his way and turn it into something beautiful.

He paddles for a knee-high lump as it approaches the contest zone, hops to his feet and has cross-stepped half-way to the nose of his board before the wave has even had a chance to think about breaking. For a moment he stalls, considers going left (travelling across the wave from surfer's right to left) but then thinks better of it and opts to go right. A couple more cross-steps and he's almost at the nose. He balances there for a few seconds and then, just before the wave whumps against the shore, scuttles back to the tail of his board to absorb the impact. His next wave is a left, but he doesn't get far before it closes out in front of him. Never mind, he's straight back out and onto another long right, this one finished off with a stylish floater into the shorebreak. Next, he's setting up yet another left, cross-stepping all the way to the nose and hanging five toes over for a gravity-defying hang five. With a few minutes of the heat still to go, his combined score for his best two rides is so convincing that the other surfers have started cheering his waves instead of trying to overhaul him.

'The way I've been taught to surf competitions,' says Parkin, over the phone from his home in Dunbar, 'is to build yourself a house. At the start you get two or three waves to get yourself a solid foundation, and then you want to start being a bit more picky. I surfed a little bit differently to that in my first heat, though, as I had to adapt to the conditions. In that heat, you couldn't really tell what the waves were going to do. You'd see one that you'd think is going to be amazing, but then it closes out or it's too fast or too slow; then you'd see one you think is pretty mediocre but somehow it works out perfectly.' His approach, then, was to minimise the chances of missing a good wave by catching as many as he could – an exhausting strategy, perhaps, but as it turned out, the right one.

In addition to that, he had the laws of physics on his side: a smaller surfer paddling a big surfboard will typically catch waves more easily than a larger surfer paddling a big surfboard. 'I suppose I did have the upper hand,' he says. 'I'm pretty light and I was on a big board, so those waves were bigger to me than they were to them.' Studying the surf carefully in advance also helped. 'I had surfed that [sand]bank at the same tide the day before,' he says, 'and I'd been watching the waves a lot before my heat. Just as I got in that left that I was catching started to work.'

Fast-forward to Day Two of the contest, and, in a building swell, Parkin surfs through the quarters and semis and into the Men's final, alongside his coach and 2022 national champion Sam Christopherson. Conditions are stormy earlier in the day, but by the time the four finalists paddle out the wind has dropped and there are beautiful, glassy shoulder-to-head-high waves rolling through the contest zone. Parkin takes full advantage, showing himself to be just as comfortable flying across powerful, hollow faces as in the previous day's ankle-slappers. In the end, it's yet another noseride on yet another left that gives him the win over Christopherson.

So – was it weird surfing against his mentor? 'Yeah, he's taught me pretty much everything,' Parkin says. 'He's given me all my knowledge about where I surf, how to read the conditions, all that. In contests though, it comes down to a bit of luck, in the end, and not mucking up on that one wave that might come to you.' Remarkably, although Parkin has previous as a shortboard competitor, winning both the Under-14 and Under-16 national titles in Thurso last year, he has only been riding a longboard for around 12 months, after buying a second-hand board crafted by veteran east coast shaper Martin McQueenie. What is it in particular that he likes about longboarding? 'I love getting to the nose,' he says, 'that feeling of getting right to the nose and getting in the pocket, I love that. When I go out on a shortboard I'm only really thinking about my progression and I just run heats in my head the whole time, but when I'm out on the longboard it's a lot chiller, a lot calmer. It's not that I like it more, I just like it in different ways.'

Scottish surfing gets its first CEO

COULD a Scottish surfer make it to the Olympics one day? Paul Stark, newly appointed CEO of the Scottish Surfing Federation, certainly isn't afraid to dream big.

22 June 2024

What a difference a couple of decades can make. In 2004 the Scottish Surfing Federation, the sport's governing body in Scotland, had been defunct for five years, after running fatally low on members, funds and committed volunteers. The scars of this period can still be seen on the SSF website – on the list of previous winners of the coveted Scottish National Surfing Championships title, dating all the way back to Bill Batten in 1973, there are no names beside the years from 1999–2004, as no contests were run during this time. In 2005, however, with surfing enjoying a resurgence in popularity, the National Championships were finally held again in Thurso, and the SSF was formally resurrected. Since then, the organisation has gone from strength to strength, reinvigorating the national contest scene, winning recognition for Scotland as an independent surfing nation and subsequently fielding teams at both the World Surfing Games and Eurosurf.

Now, with the opening of the £60 million Lost Shore artificial wave pool at Ratho only months away – the biggest sports infrastructure project in Scotland in over a decade – the SSF has appointed its first ever CEO, Paul Stark, partly to make the most of this game-changing opportunity. Given the timescales involved, you'd expect Stark to act like a man in a hurry, which he does: when we meet for coffee in central Edinburgh he's abuzz with ideas and enthusiasm. Equally, though, given his background in sustainability (the sports consultancy business he founded looks at both the environmental impact of sporting organisations and their long-term futures) he's a believer in taking a carefully considered view. The not-inconsiderable task he has set himself, then, could perhaps best be summarised as follows: get things right, but get them right quickly.

'For me,' he says, 'the main thing is to have as many conversations as possible. We all want to see a huge amount of progress within a short space of time, and with Lost Shore open I really want to have the organisation in as strong a position as it can be in order to maximise that opportunity. What we really want to make sure of, though, is that we're bringing people with us, so we want to hear from everybody because we want our aspirations as a governing body to reflect our membership. That's the most important thing.'

For all that it has achieved in the last two decades, the SSF has always been a volunteer-run organisation. In order for it to continue to flourish, Stark believes, it now needs the same kinds of structures in place as the governing bodies of more mainstream sports. 'The goal here is really to make sure that we've got a solid foundation that we can build on,' he says. 'As sport professionalises, we will need to make sure we have all those things that we should have as a national governing body in place in terms of governance and policies, the safeguarding of children, etc.'

From 2021–23, Stark worked as head of governance for the UCI Cycling World Championships in Glasgow, so he's no stranger to sporting small print. He was also head of business operations at Scottish Cycling from 2019–21, so he has an eye on the financial details too, and he sees his new role as being about growing the business side of surfing in Scotland as well as growing it as a sport. 'We have a partnership agreement in place with the Surf Lab at Edinburgh Napier University at the moment, to look at research and development,' he says, 'and we'll be looking to benefit not just the sport through that R&D but also to support Scottish businesses, start-ups and SMEs. So we're not just looking to grow the sport [in terms of participation], we're also looking to grow it through the economy, through industry as well. As the first chief exec of the sport I'd really want our impact to be far wider than the sport itself, and to make sure that we've got productive partnerships with everyone that wants to work with us.'

Clearly the partnership between the SSF and Lost Shore will be key once the resort opens in September. 'I think it's going to be a step-change,' Stark says. 'But it's an opportunity we've got to make sure we maximise. With Lost Shore open, being able to tell people we've got waves at a certain size at a certain time is going to provide an opportunity for competitions and attracting people in. . . people can turn up knowing they're going to have a certain experience. It will also provide a performance base for Scottish surfing and a place for research and development.

'The Lost Shore resort and the SSF are two completely separate organisations, but we're both looking to work in partnership for the same outcomes: to have more people involved in the sport of surfing and to have that progression pathway to get them all the way through from whatever club or surf school they attend, in whatever discipline they choose to take part in, to national and international competitions. That's what we're looking for – and with surfing's inclusion in the next three Olympic cycles, I really want to see a Scottish athlete on the podium.'

PART THREE

Freesurfing

Ian Battrick tames a
north coast sea monster

THE most intimidating surf photograph ever taken in Scottish waters? Hard to pick a winner, but the one Tim Nunn took of Ian Battrick surfing an unnamed north shore slab in January 2011 is definitely up there. It's not the height of the wave that's so threatening, more the thickness of its lip – that, and the fact that about half of it seems to be breaking below sea level. Originally from Jersey, Battrick lost three close friends in quick succession in his teens and resolved to live his life to the fullest from then on. He has since gone on to carve out an impressive career as a professional freesurfer, following waves around the world and getting paid to get his picture taken surfing them. The vast majority of surfers are freesurfers – the term really just means someone who doesn't surf in contests. To make a living from it, though, requires top tier wave-riding skills, and also a willingness to occasionally put yourself in impossible situations in order to get that one killer shot.

2 April 2011

It's no secret that the north coast of Scotland is home to some world-class surf spots. Ever since April 2006, the best wave-riders on the planet have congregated in Thurso – an unlikely surf town if ever there was one – to take part in the Coldwater Classic, a megabucks professional contest sponsored by US wetsuit company O'Neill. And they'll be up there again later this month, battling it out for points and prizes in the frigid waters of the Pentland Firth. Depending on conditions, the contest is usually held either at a reef known as Thurso East, close to the harbour entrance, which produces long, endlessly peeling walls of water in a big swell, or at Brims Ness, a point a few miles to the west where spinning liquid cylinders explode on to a shallow rocky ledge with frightening force, and where the difference between a triumphant tube ride and a brutal, bruising wipeout is measured in fractions of a second.

Thanks to the Coldwater Classic and the resulting media exposure, these two spots are now in all the guidebooks – your average 15-year-old Aussie surf nut could probably point out Thurso on a map – but for every on-the-radar gem such as Thurso East and Brims, there are still plenty of other spots up there on the wild, windswept coast of Caithness that are known only to a few hardcore locals. This winter, surf journalist and photographer Tim Nunn spent several weeks in the far north, following local surfer Chris Noble and Jersey's Ian Battrick – both sponsored by UK clothing company Finisterre – as they hunted down ship-killing waves at a time when the rest of the country was busy shovelling snow. And one of the places they surfed makes Brims look like a beginner spot.

Out of respect for the local surfing community, Nunn is keeping schtum about the precise whereabouts of this particular sea monster, but he is happy to describe the general seriousness of the situation. 'The wave actually breaks just a couple of metres from a low cliff,' he says, 'and that's what makes it tricky. It's really shallow, just a slab of barely wet rock really. The reef itself is actually quite smooth, but rock is rock – it's always hard when you hit it.'

One image of Battrick flying through a big blue barrel shows the seriousness of the wave: most of Battrick's body is well below sea level, the falling guillotine of water above his head is about as thick as a motorway overpass, and if he falls he's only got a few inches of water between him and the reef below. 'That picture was taken back in January,' says Nunn, 'one of those rare, magical Scottish winter days when there's not much wind and blazing sunshine, with a really good swell running.'

When waves get beyond a certain size they start moving so fast that paddling into them under your own steam becomes almost impossible, so Battrick was towed into this behemoth, hanging onto a rope attached to a jet ski piloted by Noble. Meanwhile, in order to get the right angle for the shot, Nunn was patiently treading water just yards from the impact zone. 'Just getting in and out of the water there is tricky,' he says. 'You have to negotiate a nasty shorebreak onto dry rock and then it's a long cold swim just to stay in position against the current – I think I swam for about three hours that day. But it's worth it when that golden moment comes along.'

Most surf photographers tend to gravitate towards warmer latitudes, where a day at the office typically involves setting up a tripod under a palm tree. Nunn, however, who studied Geography at Aberystwyth University before turning his hand to surf filming and photography, is more interested in colder climes. He has a new book out this month – appropriately titled *Numb* – which will showcase his pictures of coldwater surfing in out-of-the-way places such as Iceland and Northwest Canada. But Scotland, he assures us, will definitely be on the cover.

The Joxy Girls: in search
of a different vibe

WHEN Andy Bennetts and Malcolm Findlay wrote about the uniqueness of Scottish surf culture in their 2023 book *Surfing Scotland*, one of the factors they highlighted was a self-aware, often self-deprecating sense of humour – which perhaps makes the Joxy Girls the perfect exemplar of the Scottish surfing mindset. A band of women drawn together by their love of chasing waves in a cold climate, by picking a name that set up a direct comparison between their own less-than-glamorous surfing experiences and the carefully stage-managed image of Quiksilver's surfer-models, the Roxy Girls, they managed to have a laugh both at their own expense, and at the multinational surf brand trying to sell them gear through the medium of highly stylised images of tropical surfing perfection.

12 November 2011

To a hypnotic synth-pop soundtrack embroidered with faintly tribal-sounding, sub-Enya wailing, a group of tanned, bikini-clad young women frolic underwater like so many slow-motion, soft-focus mermaids. It could be a TV advert for a Sandals holiday resort, but these are the Roxy Girls, and this is the trailer for their instructional surf film, *Roxy – Learn to Surf NOW*. Founded in 1990, Roxy is the female arm of multinational surf apparel company Quiksilver, and these days it accounts for almost a third of the parent company's annual turnover. The Roxy Girls are the label's sponsored surfer/models, paid to travel the world, living the beach-bum dream.

The synchronised swimming continues, as does the tribal wailing, and snatches of text are flashed up on the screen: 'The Roxy

Girls . . . invite you . . . to share . . . a beautiful secret . . . learn to . . . surf NOW.' Cut to: a slow motion shot of two tanned, blonde girls giggling while tandem surfing at Waikiki. Cut to: a slow-motion shot of a solitary tanned blonde girl giggling while hugging her surfboard and drinking a Slurpee. No doubt the Roxy Girls' film had the desired effect of getting hundreds of young women all over the world into surfing, but it also had one consequence its makers could never have envisaged: the formation of Scotland's very own female surfing collective, the Joxy Girls.

Caroline Stott, Laura Carse and Sally Harris first started bumping into each other in the mid-noughties, in the cold, soggy car parks of some of the East Coast's better-known surf breaks. Delighted to discover they weren't the only women jumping into the North Sea for kicks on a regular basis, they bonded over hot drinks and chocolate bread and had soon become the focus of an unofficial all-girl surf posse with members up and down the country. 'I think at some point we had all watched the Roxy Girls' guide to surfing,' says Stott, 32, 'and we all thought it was a little bit, er . . . I don't want to say anything too negative, but absolutely nothing like learning to surf in Scotland. I mean, bikinis matching your surfboard, all that sort of stuff – we were just like: "Oh my God, that's hideous!" I think we were all just having a laugh together one night and talking about the Roxy Girls, and then one of us came up with the idea of the Joxy Girls – the Scottish equivalent.'

The idea grew legs. Stott and Co set up a Joxy Girls Facebook page, got Joxy Girls stickers for their surf vans and had Joxy Girls T-shirts printed for a group trip to a surf camp in Morocco. They've even got local surfboard shaper Jason Burnett making them surfboards with Joxy Girls logos on. 'Our ultimate aim is to make our own DVD,' says Stott, 'a spoof of the Roxy Girls' guide to surfing. We've been talking about it for ages.' On a slightly more serious note, the popularity of the Joxy Girls (120 Facebook followers and counting) suggests that they have filled an important niche in Scottish surfing – a ready-made community that aspiring girl surfers can plug into in what is still a largely male-dominated sport. 'We get a lot of people getting in touch saying, "I really want to go surfing and I heard you guys are a good crew of women surfers – can I come and surf with you sometime?"' says Stott. 'We've been back to Morocco a couple of times now, we do a big summer solstice beach party every year and we usually do an annual trip up to Lewis as well, and a trip up to the north coast.'

Add to that already-full calendar the first ever Joxy Girls Weekend, held today and tomorrow at the Innerwick Residential Centre outside Dunbar, where, in addition to surfing and beach safety sessions, there will be skateboarding, yoga, massages and makeovers. 'It's all about chatting about surfing and giving each other as many tips as we can,' says Stott. And in contrast to similar male-run events, there will be no competitive element whatsoever.

'There's a different vibe when you're in the water with other women,' says Stott. 'It's a lot more relaxed and a lot more supportive. There's no need to look macho.'

The science behind a shark
encounter at Spey Bay

SCOTLAND'S surfers may have chilly temperatures to contend with, but at least they don't have to worry about sharks. Well, they didn't think they did until 2011, when a shark seemed to have charged a surfer at Spey Bay. Happily, however, shark expert Richard Peirce was able to set the record straight.

30 September 2012

A few weeks ago in these pages I mentioned the story of Andrew Rollo, who was 'bumped' by a shark – probably a porbeagle – while surfing at Spey Bay last autumn. (Porbeagles are a lot like great whites, only smaller and less angry-looking.) I also pointed out – twice – that no one has ever been killed by a shark in UK waters, and that there have been very few cases of sharks interacting with humans in any way in this northerly neck of the woods. Still, the thought of large, carnivorous beasties cruising around the Scottish coastline in search of their dinner prompted North Sea surfer Tim Pow to write in, saying he found the whole idea 'a bit freaky' and asking me if I could look into the likelihood of his coming into contact with Jaws's little brother while bobbing about in the waves. Pow also referred me to a recent article in the Surfer's Path magazine, which suggested that sharks are more likely to visit the North Sea in the autumn because this is when grey seals have their pups. 'If this is the case,' he said, 'maybe we just need to be careful going into the seas around our coast at certain times of year.'

No Scottish surfer wants to be told to stay out of the sea in the autumn – it's when the waves tend to be at their best and when the water is at its warmest – so I got on the blower to Richard Peirce, chairman of conservation charity The Shark Trust looking for reassurance. 'I spoke to several people involved in the Spey Bay incident,' he told me. 'It almost certainly wasn't an attack, but to me it was a very, very interesting incident. The shark was probably a porbeagle, but this was very un-porbeagle-like behaviour because they're not normally investigatory animals – they normally avoid human contact. I should know: I've spent 20 years trying to film and photograph them and I know how bloody difficult it is because they always run away.'

What are the chances of a porbeagle attack off the east coast of Scotland? 'Negligible to zero,' according to Peirce. Are there any other species of shark in the North Sea that could potentially do damage to a human? 'Theoretically blue sharks may be there,' he reckons. 'They are not common and will be just about to buzz off if they are there, because they generally head south when the water goes below about 13 or 14 degrees. Makos are not unknown but they're incredibly rare these days because we've killed most of them. Most of these species are depleted to an amazing extent – we just kill too many and stick their fins in bowls of soup. So really the answer is no. These animals just don't target humans – if they did we'd have shark attacks in Britain, with the amount of surfers out there now.'

In his book, Shark Attack Britain, Peirce scours the archives for examples of attacks in UK waters but fails to find anything that resembles a Jaws-style mauling. That said, there have been accidental deaths caused by sharks – one in which a couple of Royal Navy officers tried to blow up a basking shark with plastic explosives but ended up killing themselves and the shark; one in which a boat was overturned by a basking shark and two of the passengers drowned. In the latter case, the shark was said to have charged the boat, but Peirce thinks it was probably just breaching and the boat happened to get in the way. 'That's the closest thing to a shark attack we've had in British waters as far as I can tell,' he says. 'If I were a surfer I would not be worried.'

So there you have it: surfing in the North Sea may be cold and unglamorous, but at least we don't have to worry about 'the men in grey suits' as Australian surfers sometimes refer to their shark population. That said, surfers in the Hebrides might want to consider the following analysis from Peirce: 'I am of the opinion that we get the occasional great white shark as a vagrant visitor on the west coast,' he told me. 'I've looked at about 100 incidents of claimed great white shark encounters over the last 20-odd years, of which eight remain credible post-investigation, and they're all on the west in two clusters: one is off North Cornwall, the other is around the Western Isles.'

The future of Scottish surfing, as viewed from the shoulder

WITH the benefit of hindsight, the idea that I might ever have been worried for 11-year-old Ben Larg's safety in overhead waves seems ridiculous. Three years after this session on Tiree, 14-year-old Ben was surfing 30-foot waves at Mullaghmore in Ireland; at 16 he was riding 40-foot waves at Nazare in Portugal. Back in 2016 though, none of that history had been written – he was still just a skinny little kid, out surfing thumping, hollow waves on a day when plenty of grown-up surfers seemed happy enough to watch the action from the comfort of their cars up on the dunes.

12 November 2011

On Tiree, the wind is king. Make enough visits to this almost entirely flat little island, poking its nose defiantly out into the Atlantic from beneath the skirts of the Outer Hebrides, and you soon come to appreciate its power to dictate your day. During the summer months, if the weather's sunny and still, you'll be warm enough in a T-shirt; if it's blowing more than about 20mph, though, you'll need to dress as if it's the middle of winter. (Unless, of course, you've worked out all the angles, and have managed to find yourself a rare sheltered spot to bask in, in which case you'll need to dress like an Arctic explorer on the way there, then break out the beachwear when you arrive.)

And if the wind plays a big part in the lives of civilians, for the island's small but significant surfing population it's more-or-less a deity; certainly an authority that must be obeyed. If it's blowing from the north, chances are any waves at south-facing Balephuil will be worth a look; if it's from the east, then the tricky-to-get-to Maze over on the west coast will be a good place to try; and if it's howling from the west, and if the swell's big enough, it's sometimes even possible to get a nice little peeler at south-east facing Crossapol, where – on a clear day – you can enjoy the surreal experience of paddling out towards the mountains of Mull and the mainland in order to catch waves that have travelled in from the open ocean to the west, then wrapped themselves half-way around the island to get to you.

All these spots can deliver great surf on the right day, but the most popular of them all is Balevullin – a crescent of coarse, purplish-white sand in the island's far north-western corner. Here, a solid west swell fanned by an offshore wind, can produce the kind of waves that stick in the memory for years, so on a dreich Tuesday in late June, with an eight-foot/11 second interval swell lumping in from the west and a 28mph wind blowing from the south-east, it was no surprise to see the car park above the beach busy with cars and vans, even though it wasn't exactly what your average bucket-and-spader would describe as 'beach weather'.

Out in the middle of the bay, two black dots bobbed side by side, then started paddling quickly for the horizon as a series of thick, dark bands of swell marched in out of deep water, hollowed out as they reached the edge of the sandbar and then broke with a crack and a rumble, spray pouring from their crests like smoke from a steam train. I scrambled into my wetsuit, grabbed my board and picked my way out through the swirling shorebreak, aiming a little to the left of the dots. As I drew closer I recognised them as locals Ben Larg, who won the under-14s at the Scottish Surfing Championships this year, aged just 11, and Finn MacDonald, who won the under-18s aged 15.

The last time I'd seen Ben was four years previously, on a sunny day at Balephuil. Back then, his dad, Marti, had been teaching him the basics in small, fun-sized waves, but today Ben was the one giving the masterclass. As I paddled hard to get safely over the top of a heaving eight-footer I glanced over my right shoulder and saw Ben leap effortlessly to his feet just beneath the lip of the wave, drop smoothly down its face and then come rocketing towards me as his fins converted lateral motion into down-the-line speed. The wave would have been well overhead for me, but on Ben – who isn't tall for his age – it looked positively Hawaiian. He wasn't fazed by it though – in fact, he and Finn were clearly having a blast, hooting with excitement each time another good set rolled in and the horizon turned black.

That's not to say they weren't looking out for each other; after Ben took another late drop and failed to re-appear again on the inside I found myself anxiously scanning the whitewater for any sign of a head breaking the surface and noticed Finn, sitting a few yards away, doing the same. Only when Ben had popped up with a grin and started paddling back out did Finn turn his attention back to what was happening out to sea.

After a few more waves, the pair headed in, Finn carving strong, spray-flinging turns all the way to the inside on his final ride, and I was left alone with only an inquisitive seal for company. 'That,' I said to the seal, pointing in the direction of the beach, 'was the future of Scottish surfing.' The seal looked at me for a moment, cocked its head a little to one side as if to say 'Pfft, yeah, tell me something I don't know,' and disappeared with a splash of its flippers.

Andrew Robertson's dream
summer job on Tiree

THE surf hut referenced in this story was built at Balevullin on Tiree by Marti and Iona Larg as a home for their Blackhouse Watersports business, but it also serves as a de facto clubhouse and changing room for the island's small but dedicated surfing community. Not long after this story was published, it became the subject of a fierce debate over planning permission, with some locals wanting it removed and others arguing that it should stay. News of the debate spread so far beyond the shores of Tiree that I even received a rare desk-side visit from the then-editor of The Scotsman, Ian Stewart, who had decided to make it the subject of the paper's leader column. Happily, the hut is still standing at time of writing, allowing surfers to shelter from the rain while checking the surf, just as Andrew Robertson and I did in 2016.

16 July 2016

Andrew Robertson and I are sitting in the new surf hut on the beach at Balevullin, on the west coast of Tiree, sheltering from a sudden, heavy rain shower. Out in the bay, the swell that's been lighting up the island for several days is still in the healthy four to-six-foot range, but it's being made lumpy and unpredictable by a stiff cross-shore breeze. Every now and then a good-looking wave hits the outside sandbar and rumbles through with something resembling a rideable wall to it, but on the whole it's a bit of a mess. None of which seems to have put even the tiniest dent in Robertson's infectious enthusiasm. 'On a good day, when the wind's offshore and the swell's from the right direction, you can sometimes get amazing barrels over there by the rocks,' he says, pointing through the hut's rain-streaked window towards the far corner of the bay. He smiles at the thought of it – it's the smile of somebody who knows that the next time the waves out here get really good, he'll almost certainly be around to take full advantage.

Robertson currently has what may well be the best summer job in Scotland. Working for Tiree's Blackhouse Watersports, his daily grind consists of giving surf lessons to tourists, welcoming all-comers to the hut and generally keeping it neat and tidy. Then, in his down-time, he's free to surf his brains out. He has, he says, been drinking a lot of coffee, presumably to keep him going through multiple surfs each day. At the start of the summer he was staying at the island's hostel and working as a cleaner. He quite liked meeting all the different people passing through to begin with, he says, but after a while having the same conversations over and over again got to be a bit of a chore. Now he's living in a caravan within sight of the surf at Balevullin and he's much happier – as you would be, if you were based within spitting distance of one of the best surf spots in Scotland, were still in your teens, and still had a whole summer stretching out in front of you, promising nothing but waves, waves and more waves. If I sound jealous, it's probably because I am.

To describe Robertson, who hails from St Andrews, as a pro-
digious talent is probably under-selling it. He blew minds in the
Scottish surfing world at the Gathering of the Clans event at
Thurso last October when, still aged just 17, he didn't just take
home the junior title but the men's open title as well, defeating
big-hitters Mark Boyd and Chris Clarke in the process. What's
even more remarkable is that by then he'd already represented his
country at senior level, travelling to Punta Rocas, Peru in 2014
to compete for Team Scotland at the ISA World Surfing Games.

This year, however, he's been unlucky – before landing the
dream job on Tiree, that is. First, a bout of pneumonia meant
he couldn't compete in the Scottish Surfing Championships in
April, where national team selections are made; then, to make
matters worse, he broke his arm while skateboarding – a nasty
injury at the elbow that took a lengthy and frustrating period of
rehab to put right. Not that the smashed elbow has put him off
skateboarding – he still talks animatedly about his high-speed
downhill adventures, particularly at Rest and Be Thankful (not
on the A-road itself, dodging traffic, but on an equally steep private road nearby).

Later in the afternoon the rain stops, the wind dies down
and the surf begins to sort itself out again. By the time I get
my act together and paddle out there are already three Scottish
surfing champions in the water – Tiree residents Ben Larg and
Finn MacDonald plus Robertson, who seems to be picking off
long, winding lefts at the rate of about one every couple of minutes. Then, as if things weren't already intimidating enough for
any mere mortals in the line-up, Olympic snowboarder Lesley
McKenna comes powering out to join us, expertly duckdiv-
ing through one of the larger sets of the day. I decide it's time
to leave the sideways sliding to the pros, so I ride a wave back

to shore, grab my camera and point it out to sea, just in time to see Robertson drop into a picture-perfect left. He darts down the line, carefully building speed as the wave walls up in front of him; then, as he reaches the end section, he banks hard at the bottom and powers off the top, throwing the tail of his board through a graceful, spray-flinging arc. This year's Gathering of the Clans is due to be held on Tiree in late August; if Robertson doesn't do well – on what will by then be as good as home turf – I'll eat my wax.

History boy:
Ben Larg goes big in Ireland

THIS was the point at which everything changed for Ben Larg. Before he caught and rode this monster wave at Mullaghmore, he was just another 14-year-old kid who wanted to be a big wave surfer one day. Afterwards, he was a big wave surfer. Simple as that.

11 October 2019

The giant waves that break off Mullaghmore Head in Ireland's County Sligo are as serious as you'll find anywhere in the world. Last winter, experienced local surfer John Monahan nearly drowned there after breaking his femur and two ribs during a wipeout. In 2017, the surf photographer Ian Mitchinson says he told himself 'to brace for death' after he was pinned underwater by a monster wave. The surf forecasting website Magic Seaweed describes the spot as 'a savage, shallow, reefbreak' that 'handles any size swell, producing massive tubes, but needs to be well overhead to break clear of exposed rocks.' So for Tiree surfer Ben Larg, still aged just 14, to turn up at Mullaghmore earlier this week and ride a wave estimated to be around 30-feet high, almost beggars belief.

The reigning under-18 Scottish Surfing Champion, Larg has already represented Scotland in international contests in the Azores, Japan and Portugal but recently set his sights on surfing big waves in Ireland. He spent much of the last month training there with big wave specialists Peter Conroy and Ollie O'Flaherty, and after several failed attempts due to weather to surf another spot called Aileen's, which breaks beneath the spectacular Cliffs of Moher, on Tuesday Larg took a trip to witness the even bigger waves at Mullaghmore. Conditions were near-perfect, with a long-interval swell and offshore winds, and Larg was supported by big wave surfers Conroy, O'Flaherty and Dylan Stott.

'I'd told my Mum and Dad that I would just be watching so they didn't come along,' Larg says, 'but after a few hours watching from the jet ski in the channel, Dylan Stott asked me if I wanted to be towed into a wave. I couldn't miss the opportunity to catch a wave.

'It was my dream to surf big waves in Ireland and I'm so happy I got to surf Mullaghmore. I want to thank all of the Irish surfers I've met for helping me to do this. I can't wait to surf more big waves in the future and I hope that this can help me to attract a sponsor.'

The 30-foot wave Larg caught makes him the youngest ever to surf a wave that size at Mullaghmore, and images of his ride might remind surfers of a certain age of the famous '60 Days that Shook the Pacific' *Surfer* magazine cover from 1994 which showed another 14 year-old, Jay Moriarity, surfing a similar sized-wave at Californian big wave spot Mavericks. The only difference:

Left. An 1897 portrait of Princess Victoria Ka'iulani Cleghorn, heir to the Hawaiian throne and perhaps the first Scottish surfer. (Wikicommons)

Above. Neva MacDonald-Haig and friends riding their 'coffin-lid' surfboards at Machrihanish in the 1930s. (Courtesy of the MacDonald-Haig family)

Brian Morgan, Sandy Mathers and Dave Killoh at Aberdeen Beach, where they first surfed in the 1960s. (Simon Price)

Top. Bill Batten, Ian Wishart and Andy Bennetts at Shackleton's Pub, Edinburgh, 2018. (Courtesy of Matt Brown / MBP Productions)

Above. Seven-time Scottish National Surfing Champion Iain Masson at Thurso East, 1994. (Andy Bennetts)

Right. Vince Attfield in Shetland, where he and a few others started surfing in the early 1990s. (Dave Donaldson)

World surfing champion Sunny Garcia of Hawaii warming up for the 2008 O'Neill Highland Open at Brims Ness. (Roger Cox)

Mark Cameron's last-ditch attempt to progress from the first round of the 2008 O'Neill Highland Open. (Chris Laurens)

Megan Mackay, the first Scot ever to win an international surfing competition: the 2017 Nordic Surf Games. (Malcolm Anderson)

Chris Noble, six-time Scottish National Surfing Champion, deep in the barrel at Thurso East. (Malcom Anderson)

Mark Boyd, 'a full-blooded power surfing act', fully committed at Thurso East. (Malcolm Anderson)

Ansel Parkin claiming the men's longboard title at the Scottish National Surfing Championships, Pease Bay, 2024. (Malcolm Anderson)

Ian Battrick looking for an exit, somewhere in northern Scotland. (Tim Nunn)

The Joxy Girls at Seacliff, East Lothian. (Janeanne Gilchrist)

Marti Larg, Ben Larg and Andrew Robertson at Balevullin on Tiree, July 2016. (Roger Cox)

Top. Ross Ryan painting on the north coast during his 2021–22 'Crinan to Catterline' voyage. (Courtesy of the artist)

Above. Installation view of Laura Maynard's *Wave Migration* exhibition at An Lanntair, Stornoway. (John Maclean / courtesy of An Lanntair)

Right. Colin MacLeod and Will Brawn swapping surfboards for studio time on Lewis in 2015. (Mike Guest)

Top. Craig Sutherland, owner of Suds Surf School in Sandend and head coach of Scotland's junior surf team. (Mike Guest)

Above left. Brian and Sarah Stark outside their Boardwise surf and snow shop after it was gutted by fire in 2016. (Roger Cox)

Above right. Sam Christopherson at the Belhaven Surf Centre near Dunbar, home to his Coast to Coast surf school. (Mike Guest)

Left. Alasdair Steele of environmental charity Surfers Against Sewage at Pease Bay, October 2012. (Roger Cox)

Right. Andy Hadden, founder of Scotland's first artificial wave pool, Lost Shore, at Ratho near Edinburgh. (Courtesy of Lost Shore)

Below. An aerial view of the Lost Shore wave pool, shortly after it was completed in 2024. (Courtesy of Lost Shore)

Ben Larg competing at the 2025 Big Wave Challenge at Nazaré, Portugal.
(Damien Poullenot / courtesy of the World Surf League)

Moriarity's ride ended in a horrific wipeout; Larg rode his wave all the way to the channel.

Conroy, who is a member of the Irish Tow Surf Rescue Club, says, 'Surfing big waves is more of a mental thing than a physical thing. Having the right mindset and courage to face what could potentially hurt you is what it's all about. After training with Ben and seeing his ability in the water and out, I felt great seeing him manhandle such a good wave in Mullaghmore. He rode the wave very, very well and you could see the confidence in his surfing the whole wave. I'm very happy to have met Ben and spark the love for bigger waves. He did an absolutely brilliant job at waiting and observing the wave and wanted to try it. And I'm very happy he did. I can't wait to see him out there again.'

The wave was caught on film by production company Urbancroft Films, who have been following Larg and his family for the last three years for a feature-length documentary, *Riding the Wave*. The film has been supported by Screen Scotland and is due for release in 2020. Martyn Robertson is the producer and director of the film. 'We've been following Ben's story since he was 12,' he says, 'and this wave tops off what was already an amazing story. Ben and his family are completely inspirational and we're really looking forward to completing the film and releasing it in 2020.'

'As ithers see us': An Aussie take on the Scottish surfing experience

THESE days, professional Australian freesurfer and filmmaker Torren Martyn is best-known for his award-winning 2023 film *Calypte* – a feature-length adventure in which he and surf scribe

Aiyana Powell (neither of whom have much experience with boats) spend a year sailing from Thailand to East Indonesia on the titular 35-foot yacht, courting disaster and surfing dream-like waves along the way. Before *Calypte*, however, there was *Lost Track Atlantic* – a series of short surf films Martyn made with his friend Ishka Folkwell, charting their Transit van adventures across Europe and Africa. The Scottish episode was filmed in 2019, the same year Martyn was voted the most stylish surfer in the world by US magazine *Surfer*. Watching his unique, laid-back interpretation of some of Scotland's premier surf spots was an education.

8 May 2021

'It's so miserable out there!' moans Aussie surfer Torren Martyn, still half-asleep in bed as an Atlantic squall batters the outside of his camper van. 'And it's so warm in here too!' Martyn and his filmmaker buddy Ishka Folkwell are parked up on the edge of a low cliff, overlooking a deserted but stunning surf spot on Scotland's north coast, and Martyn is giving voice to a dilemma that will be familiar to anyone who has ever ridden waves in this part of the world: to stay inside where it's warm and comfortable, or to pull on a wetsuit and brave the elements. Given that Martyn honed his skills in the balmy waters of Byron Bay, it's hardly surprising that he's a little reluctant to leave his warm bed and jump into the Pentland Firth, but it isn't long before he's suited and booted (and gloved, and hooded) and paddling out into chunky, barreling waves. What follows is one of the most memorable scenes from the recently-released first episode of *Lost Track Atlantic* – a four-part travelogue, filmed in 2019, in which the duo pick up a clapped out Ford Transit van in England and then use it to explore the prime surf zones of Ireland and Scotland before heading south towards the tropical waves of West Africa.

To begin with, Folkwell focuses on the wave itself (they don't name the spot so we won't either), showing in slow motion how it lumps up out of deep water when it hits the edge of the reef, how the lip feathers as it's caught by the offshore wind, and then how it folds over itself to form a perfect, reeling cylinder. Surfers will also note that the foam explosion thrown up by the breaking wave is almost twice the height of the wave itself: a tell-tale sign that the water in the impact zone is board-breakingly shallow. Then, back in real time, we see Martyn paddling hard for a wave, skimming down its face and ducking under the lip as it morphs into a huge, circular waterfall. And if he seems to be drifting casually along in the barrel, rather than frantically pumping for speed as a pro contest surfer might do, that's partly down to his choice of surf craft; because, while most of the rest of the surfing world remains obsessed with three-fin surfboards, Martyn favours twin-fins, last dominant on the pro tour in the early 1980s. These boards lend themselves to a more mellow, graceful style of surfing, and so, even if some of the waves Martyn surfs in *Lost Track Atlantic* will be familiar to viewers, the way he interprets them probably won't be.

'O wad some Pow'r the giftie gie us,' wrote the Bard, 'To see oursels as ithers see us!' That's not quite what we get from *Lost Track Atlantic* – there's not much attempt to engage with Scottish surfers or Scottish surfing culture.

What we do get, though, is an outsider's view of Scotland as a surf destination, and through the eyes of Martyn and Folkwell, Scotland looks pretty darn good. Scottish surfers tend to think of warm-water locations like Australia and Hawaii as 'exotic' but these are places where surfing is mainstream – as far as most of the surfing world is concerned, Scotland is exotic. 'We'd hardly rolled off the ferry and we were stunned by the beauty of Scotland,' says Martyn in voiceover. 'The snow-capped mountains, the freezing weather . . . it really felt like we were such a long way from home.'

There have been some magical Scottish surf flicks over the years, from Mark Lumsden's *Cold Rush*, released in the early Noughties, to Malcolm Anderson and Rups's 2017 film *01847* (named after the dialling code for Thurso, in case you were wondering). On the whole, though, these films have tended to be homegrown productions featuring local surfers, so it's always good to see what wave-riders from elsewhere make of the place.

The climax of *Lost Track Atlantic: Episode One* is a sequence showing Martyn surfing Thurso East. Thanks to the series of pro contests held at the break in the Noughties, its contours will now be familiar to surfers the world over, but watching Martyn tackle it at double-overhead on one of his channel-bottomed twin-fins is to see it through fresh eyes. His bottom-turns are so long-drawn-out you fear he'll be hammered by the whitewater long before he's able to pivot back up into the face of the wave, and when he stalls for a tube it seems like an age before he's able to re-establish forward momentum. Somehow, though, his casual-yet-radical approach works – better than works: makes you wonder if the aggressive aesthetic that currently dominates the sport of surfing is really as good as it gets.

After making it back to Thurso harbour, where Folkwell has been filming him, Martyn struggles to say, 'My face is all numb!' 'You can't even talk properly!' laughs Folkwell. 'But that was great fun,' Martyn sort-of says, wiping his frozen face with a wetsuit glove, 'I got it all to myself, hey? That was unreal.' And so he nails another great truism of Scottish surfing: the cold may be brutal at times, but at least it keeps the crowds down.

North coast slab hunting
with Nathan Florence

AS PARADOXICAL as it sounds, when it comes to big wave surfing, size isn't necessarily everything. Measured from peak to trough, the monsters Ben Larg and Hawaii's Nathan Florence tackled on Scotland's north coast in 2022 were never going to win any 'biggest wave of the winter' competitions. In terms of risk factor, though, due to the shallowness of the reef and the lack of rescue options, they were off the charts. Also of note in this interview: the reference to Larg signing a contract with Red Bull, making him Scotland's first ever professional surfer.

26 November 2022

When I hear that Scottish big wave surfer Ben Larg is out of the water due to a burst eardrum, I assume it's because he's taken a monster wipeout. This, after all, is the teen sensation who rode giant waves at Mullaghmore in Ireland aged just 14 and lived to tell the tale, and who surfed super-size Nazaré in Portugal last winter aged just 16, forming a tow-in partnership with established big wave legend Nic Von Rupp. As it turns out, however, his injury, while surfing-related, has nothing to do with getting on the wrong side of Mother Ocean.

Back in Portugal for another winter season, and surfing a small-wave warm-up session at Nazaré, he got into an altercation with another surfer. 'I actually got in a fight, or, at least, a guy picked a fight with me,' he says. 'He dropped in on a wave of mine, he was a bit older and he and all his mates ganged up on me. He ended up punching me just in the side of the ear and burst my eardrum. I never threw a punch at anyone – I was just walking backwards trying to calm the situation. It was a bit unlucky, but I guess sometimes surfers can be a bit aggressive. It was so unusual, it was the first time I've had any hassle in the water because I'm always super-respectful to the local guys when I'm surfing their spots.'

The doctors have told him to stay out of the water for two-to-three weeks, so he's resigned to missing out on any imminent big wave action. In the meantime, though, the 17-year-old has plenty of other projects on the go, not least working on plans for his new film series, *Ben Larg: Beyond the Island*, the first instalment of which has just been released on the Magic Seaweed website. The island in the title is the Isle of Tiree in the Inner Hebrides, where Larg grew up and learned to surf, and the new series will chart his adventures further afield while introducing viewers to some of the surfers he meets along the way. The first episode, *Ride the Line*, finds him on the north coast of Scotland in the company of another islander, Hawaiian Nathan Florence, brother of world champ John John, and one of the most respected big wave specialists in the business. With a large and unruly swell running, the original plan had been for Larg and Florence to meet up at a little-surfed reef-break to the west of Thurso and use Larg's jet ski to tow each other into the thick, barrelling waves exploding over a barely-covered rock shelf. When the ski refused to start, however, it looked like the gig was off – until Florence showed up, took a quick look at the sketchy conditions, and decided they should try paddling into waves under their own steam. Big wave surfers don't just use jet skis to help them catch waves, they also use them to get safely outside the impact zone to where the waves are breaking, and to make rescues when things go wrong. Florence's suggestion, then, was something of a gauntlet thrown down, so it was impressive that Larg decided to follow his lead. And thanks to the way the film is shot and edited by Antoine Couturier and Sam Howard of Northern Front – focusing as much on the hazardous journey off the rocks and through the breaking surf to the line-up as on the actual surfing – you don't need to be an experienced surfer to understand the magnitude of what's being attempted.

'When we rocked up to that wave I was pretty hesitant to surf it,' says Larg. 'The swell wasn't really from the right direction and the wind was all over the place – it was huge, as well, massive – but as soon as Nathan rocked up he was like "right, let's go!"'

'I'm never, ever scared when I'm surfing, like when I go to Nazaré I'm always super calm, but that day I was feeling a bit nervous. I was just like, "Ah, I'm gonna take it easy, take a slow paddle-out." I never got a proper wave, but it was great to watch Nathan surf – he's probably the best slab surfer in the world.'

While Larg may have had a difficult time on that particular day, the two surfers both scored good waves at the ever-reliable reef at Thurso East on their north coast trip, and the tail-end of the film shows them cutting loose there (and at other nearby spots) with locals Finn MacDonald (who has moved there from Tiree) and Craig McLachlan. For the next film in the series, Larg says the plan is for Couturier and Howard to visit him in Nazaré – a place where he is evidently starting to feel more at home, in spite of the recent surf-rage incident. Partly this is because he recently signed a sponsorship deal with Red Bull, who have a big presence in the town. 'That was a big one for me,' he says, 'a dream come true. The second day after I got to Nazaré, I knew I was going to be meeting the crew from Red Bull. We went out for dinner and the manager of Red Bull UK, Harry [Drnek], said "Oh, we've got a surprise for you" . . . so that was pretty cool.'

Back to where it all began

WHEN Ben Larg caught his huge, career-making wave at Mullaghmore in Ireland in 2019, he was towed into it by a jet ski; five years later, he returned to see if he could ride a few giants there using his own paddle power.

2 November 2024

In 2019, Scottish surfer Ben Larg, then aged just 14, exploded onto the big wave scene by riding a 30-foot behemoth at Mullaghmore Head in County Sligo on the west coast of Ireland. Filmmaker Martyn Robertson was on hand to capture the moment, and it became the climax of his award-winning feature-length documentary *Ride The Wave* – an intimate record of Larg's teenage quest to surf ever-bigger waves, which premiered at the London Film Festival in 2021. Since then, Larg has gone on to carve out an impressive career as a professional big wave surfer, signing a contract with action sports brand Red Bull in 2022; and earlier this month, almost exactly five years on from that life-changing moment at Mullaghmore, he returned to the place where he first made a name for himself, chasing yet another super-sized swell. Whereas he was towed into his famous 2019 wave by a jetski, however, this time he set out to catch waves under his own steam.

'This was the first time I'd ever paddled Mullaghmore,' he says over the phone from his home on the Isle of Tiree. 'I got a few tow waves and a few paddle waves.' Tow-in surfing makes it easier for surfers to catch giant waves, as they are able to begin each ride travelling at speed and already standing up. Conventional surfing, by contrast, requires the surfer to generate forward momentum using their own paddle-power, then jump to their feet as they drop down the wave face. Unsurprisingly, surfing giant waves in this way tends to carry a higher risk of injury. 'I got pretty flogged out there,' says Larg, although thankfully he came through the session uninjured. 'On one of the waves I fell just before the really heavy bit where it starts breaking, and I got pushed super-deep. There's this sort of ledge at Mullaghmore and if you get carried over it then you get pushed down over the other side, so that's what happened – I felt myself sinking after a little while, so I was like "oh no, this is not good."'

Larg almost didn't make it to Ireland in time for the giant swell which hit Mullaghmore on Saturday 19 October. 'I was actually at the Bristol Wave doing a training camp for young kids with [pro surfers] Jordi Smith and Johanne Defay,' he says. 'I asked my manager, "can I go to Ireland for the swell at Mullaghmore?" and he was like, "OK, on you go then", so I kind of skived off. On the Saturday morning I got a 3am flight from Bristol to Dublin, drove straight from Dublin to Mullaghmore, and I was surfing by ten. So yeah – it was a pretty hectic day, but it was worth it.' Such is the life of the professional big wave surfer. 'You can never really plan anything in surfing,' says Larg. 'You can kind of plan your year, and you've got a rough idea of where you might be, but it's chaos – sort of organised chaos.'

Earlier in October, Larg and his Australian tow-in partner Ned Hart were at a different big wave spot in Ireland – the notorious slab called Riley's near Lahinch in County Clare. The waves here might not have been as big as those at Mullaghmore when measured from peak-to-trough, but if anything they were more dangerous, due both to the shallowness of the water and the remoteness of the location. 'I think the swell was about 12–14 feet with a 16–20 second period,' says Larg, 'so that just translates into massive surf. There were 10–15ft faces, but even though that doesn't sound so big, at that wave in particular it's just so shallow and so heavy that it's a different sort of size – it's really more about how wide it breaks. The locals were saying it wasn't necessarily the biggest ever at Riley's, but maybe the most gnarly. It was all over the place.'

The approach to Riley's by land involves climbing down a huge cliff, then traversing a slippery, treacherous reef; however, Larg and Hart were using a jetski to tow each other into waves, so getting to the spot was even harder. 'To get the skis in there,' says Larg, 'you're driving for 20 minutes around this huge head-land, and in a big swell you're going in and out of these massive troughs. Then there's this little gully in the rock you have to shoot through before you get to Riley's. You can drive all the way round the headland, but to cut time there's this gap in the rock. Obviously when there's a mad swell running you've got to time it right and hopefully make it through to the other side.' Once they reached the break, Larg and Hart thought long and hard before attempting to catch a wave, due to the magnitude of the swell. 'We almost called it off,' says Larg, 'but we hung around and watched it for about an hour and then Ned was like, "Right, I'll get a couple of waves." I towed him onto one and then we pretty much never stopped after that. The boys on the beach were all like "Naa, we're not surfing, this is too crazy", but they jumped in for a few after that.'

One of the surfers who came out to join Larg and Hart that day was Hawaiian big wave expert Nathan Florence, brother of three-time world champion John John, who Larg has surfed with previously on the north coast of Scotland. In the YouTube video he released shortly after the session, he described conditions as 'huge . . . awesome, and scary'. As a general rule, if the Hawaiians are calling it scary, it probably is.

PART FOUR
Culture

Lessons in cultural fusion with
Edinburgh surf band The Nukes

THE early 1960s heyday of instrumental surf music may have
been short-lived, snuffed out by the arrival of The Beatles and
The Rolling Stones, but in America and elsewhere, along with
films like *Gidget* and *Beach Party* it was part of a winning cultural
formula that inspired countless thousands of inlanders to head
to the coast. Half a century later, in a roundabout way, it was
still working its magic in Scotland. Mark Carr of Edinburgh surf
band The Nukes didn't come to the music through surfing, but
found surfing through his love of the music. An instrumental
surf band from Leith? It sounded so unlikely that, when a copy
of The Nukes' second album *The Scars of Tuskar* landed on my
desk in 2009, I had to find out more.

12 December 2009

Few sounds are as evocative as the reverby twang of the surf guitar,
and for a fleeting moment in the early 1960s that twang became
sonic shorthand for an entire subculture – not just in Southern
California, where it originated, but all over the world. Even today,
just a few bars of surf instrumentals such as *Wipe Out* by the
Surfaris or *Misirlou* by Dick Dale and his Del Tones are enough
to transport the listener to a simple, carefree world of sun-kissed
beach parties, roadside diners and block-long cars with ridiculous

tail fins. Listen very carefully and you can almost smell the surf wax, the marshmallows, the smoke from a driftwood fire.

Of course, like all golden ages, this one didn't last long. In 1964, four cocky Scousers calling themselves The Beatles touched down on North American soil, bagged a spot on The Ed Sullivan Show and changed the course of music history forever. But instrumental surf rock didn't die following the so-called 'British Invasion' – it just went underground, where it waited patiently to be rediscovered by future generations. When Quentin Tarantino decided to soundtrack his hit 1994 film *Pulp Fiction* with surf classics including *Misirlou* and *Bustin' Surfboards* by the Tornadoes, he inspired a whole new generation of surf instrumental stylists, from Russia's Gulag Tunes to Croatia's Bambi Molesters and Slovenia's Bitch Boys. (And no, I didn't make up any of those names.)

In 2005 Scotland got in on the act too, when Edinburgh-based drummer and trumpet player Mark Carr got together with bass guitarist Derek McKenzie and, later, baritone guitarist Mark Hunter to form The Nukes. Given the niche-ness of their chosen medium, The Nukes' debut release, 2007's *Picnic in Peking*, did pretty well: Phill Jupitus played one of the tracks, *Bawheid Stomp*, on his radio show, the great Dick Dale declared The Nukes 'very, very cool' and they even got a coveted support slot with Tarantino's beloved Japanese all-girl surf band, the 5678s.

And now The Nukes are back. New album *The Scars of Tuskar* is already in the shops (well, in selected shops – try Elvis Shakespeare on Edinburgh's Leith Walk if you're trying to track down a copy) and the official launch party is due to take place at the city's Tron Tavern on Wednesday. Carr describes this latest long-player as 'more Russian or Slavic-sounding' than *Picnic in Peking*, 'with the bass much higher in the mix'. Stand-out tracks include *Murmansk Shoreleave* and *Krasimira Goes West*.

'The album was produced in Edinburgh by Steven Watkins,' says Carr. 'We recorded 11 songs in two days – played 'em live and if something wasn't right by the third take we'd go on to something else and maybe come back to it later.'

Famously, the Beach Boys didn't surf (well, apart from Dennis Wilson) but members of many early 1960s surf instrumental bands did. Bob Berryhill, original guitarist with the Surfaris, learned to surf on a family holiday to Hawaii when he was 13; Dick Dale still surfs today at the grand old age of 72. Until last month, though, nobody in The Nukes had ever given the sport of kings a go, so Carr, reasoning 'if I don't do it now, I'll never do it' booked himself in for a lesson on a popular beach just down the coast from Edinburgh, and now, it seems, he's well and truly caught the bug. 'I wish I'd got into it 20 years ago,' he says. 'I really liked it – just being in the sea, you know? My first wave, I totally caught it and went screaming in towards the shore. And then, right at the very end of the session, I managed to get up on the board. I was only up on my feet for a few seconds and then I fell off, but for a second there I was living the dream.' Did he have Nukes tunes playing in his head as he flew towards the beach? 'No, but I could definitely see what all the fuss was about. I went back last weekend – it was freezing, so I think that's probably me for the winter – but I'm going to carry on with it next year.'

It may have enjoyed a spike in popularity in recent years, but surf instrumental music is unlikely to make anybody rich or famous. Carr says he and the other Nukes are fine with that – they're happy to continue doing their thing for a small audience of diehard fans. 'It'd be nice to be included in a few film soundtracks, though,' muses Carr. Scottish surf film makers on the lookout for an authentic soundtrack, look no further.

Through the Whisky Barrel:
a film to unite Scotland's surf tribes

IN HIS 2011 film *Through the Whisky Barrel*, Allyn Harper combined footage of some of Scotland's best homegrown surfers with clips of travelling pros like Sunny Garcia and John John Florence visiting the north coast. By doing this he demonstrated two things: 1) that Scotland was undeniably home to some world class waves; 2) that its best surfers weren't a million miles away from riding them as well as the athletes on the world tour.

31 October 2011

Surf films have mutated in all kinds of different directions over the years, but in the beginning they were effectively the moving-picture equivalent of slide shows – a way of replaying epic sessions both for the benefit of the people who were there and for those who weren't. In the 1950s and 1960s, pioneering backyard cinematographers like Bud Browne would cut together footage of surfing at well-known breaks in California and Hawaii, book a slot at the local cinema (or gymnasium, or crematorium) and then charge members of the tribe a few cents apiece to chow down on popcorn and watch one another's rides. The atmosphere would often be anarchic – arch prankster Miki Dora once let a jar of moths loose in a screening held by big-wave legend Greg Noll, with unfortunate results for the projector – but at least there was a sense of community at these events, a sense of like-minded souls coming together to share their love of the ocean.

It's much easier to watch a surf movie today than it was back then – after a period in which they were mostly sold on VHS and then DVD format, many of the big surf companies are now putting films straight online, where aspiring wave-riders from Iceland to Indonesia can watch them for free from the comfort of their bedrooms. But with this ease of access, you can't help feeling that something's been lost somewhere. Sure, the message boards on surf-related websites can be entertaining enough, but they're no substitute for trash-talkin', popcorn-flingin' human interaction.

So in the light of all this, it warms the cockles somewhat to see Aberdeen-based surfer and graphic designer Allyn Harper releasing his new film *Through The Whisky Barrel* at the Granite City's Belmont Cinema today – the first time, as far as he knows, that a Scottish surf film featuring Scottish surfers will ever have been shown on a big screen in Scotland.

'I wanted to do a project that would bring Scottish surfers together,' he says. 'I often feel that we're all kind of doing our own thing – everyone just goes surfing, then goes back to their normal life.'

This community spirit extends to the way the film was produced: Harper invited anyone who felt like it to submit footage of their best sessions and then edited the clips together, interspersing the action with interviews with pioneering Caithness surfers like Pat Kiernan and Grant Coghill. 'I opened it up to other people because I was finding that a lot of friends would have a handful of really good clips of amazing surfing, but they wouldn't have enough to actually do something with it,' says Harper. 'So I asked everyone I knew for their clips, and people were really keen to get involved.'

Gerard Butler takes method acting to new heights in Chasing Mavericks

IN 2003, the celebrated US big wave surfer Jay Moriarity died in a freediving accident; 10 years later, the Hollywood movie *Chasing Mavericks* was released, telling his remarkable story, with Scottish actor Gerard Butler playing his mentor Frosty Hesson.

Unfortunately *Chasing Mavericks* didn't reveal itself to be a cinematic masterpiece when it opened in the UK, but Jonny Weston certainly captured Moriarity's passion and determination in the lead role, and Butler nailed Hesson's mixture of frustration, anger and disbelief as it becomes increasingly obvious that this kid just isn't going to leave him alone until he gets a chance to ride giant waves. Sure, some of the dialogue was a bit much, but given the long history of underachieving surf films, the whole shebang could have been a lot worse. Don't just take my word for it though. The great US critic Roger Ebert wrote it had been 'made with more care and intelligence than many another film starting with its template might have been.'

2 July 2013

You'd think Hollywood and surfing would be a match made in heaven – surfing, after all, is one of the most cinematic sports there is. But no. Every time a mass market surf drama gets the green light it always seems to end in farce. Remember *Point Break*? The film that gave us such intelligently crafted lines as 'Surfing's the source, man' and 'Speak into the microphone, squid brain'? Or what about *Surf Ninjas*? The 1993 idiot-fest in which three young surfers growing up in LA return to their Pacific island homeland, do chop-socky battle with an evil mastermind wearing a comedy mask and – to quote the toe-curling, dude-speak trailer – 'basically kick some ass'? *Blue Crush*? The less said about that one the better. *Surf Nazis Must Die*? Deliberately, almost heroically rubbish.

No, the only surf film marketed at non-surfers that could be described as anything like an artistic success is *Big Wednesday*, and although it's developed something of a cult following in recent years, when it was first released in 1978 it was a box office flop of catastrophic proportions. The critics were harsh, too. Reviewing the film for the *New York Times*, Janet Maslin gleefully shredded the acting with the immortal line: 'Barbara Hale . . . is quite unconvincing as Mr Katt's mother. This is a faux pas of no mean eminence; after all, Miss Hale actually is Mr Katt's mother.'

Under the circumstances, then, it's a minor miracle that *Chasing Mavericks* – the latest surf film to roll off the Hollywood production line – ever made it past the pitching stage. Bravely ignoring the form book, however, 20th Century Fox saw fit to pump an estimated $20 million into it and as of next Friday it's coming to a multiplex near you.

Set in California in the early 90s and starring Scotland's Gerard Butler, the film tells the true story of the late, great Jay Moriarity (Jonny Weston), a 16-year-old determined to surf the monster waves breaking at a spot called Mavericks just outside Half Moon Bay. Butler plays Frosty Hesson, one of only a handful of surfers with the skills necessary to ride the place, who eventually agrees to take the youngster under his wing.

Chasing Mavericks was released in the US last autumn, and the reviews on the other side of the pond have been less than glowing. According to one, although the action sequences are 'gorgeous,' whenever the film goes ashore 'it becomes a half-baked coming-of-age cheesefest – think *The Karate Kid* with wetsuits.' Certainly Butler's character has to spout some horrendous, hippy-dippy dialogue. One of his pearls of wisdom is as follows: 'We all come from the sea, but we are not all of the sea. Those of us who are, we children of the tides, must return to it again and again, until the day we don't come back leaving only that which was touched along the way.' Master Yoda could hardly have put it better.

Trouble is, deep down I really want this film to be good. Partly this is because Butler nearly drowned during filming on location at Mavericks, and anyone who's prepared to take method acting to those kinds of extremes deserves to be in a decent movie. Mostly, though, it's because Moriarity was an inspirational surfer, and he shouldn't have his life story presented to the world in a second-rate film.

Like a lot of surfers, I first became aware of Moriarity in the spring of 1994, thanks to a heart-stopping photo on the cover of *Surfer* magazine. Riding a red, yellow and green board, he was pictured at the frothy summit of a heaving, dark-green, 30-foot death-wave at Mavericks, and it was clear that he was in trouble. Rather than pointing down towards the bottom of the wave, the nose of his board had been caught by the howling offshore wind, and was pointing alarmingly towards the sky. His outstretched arms suggested that he was already in freefall, and that in a couple of seconds he would be deep underwater, being rolled like an ant in a washing machine. The really striking thing about the picture, though, was the caption: 'Sixteen year-old Jay Moriarity drops into history at Mavericks'. Sixteen? What had driven someone so young to surf waves like that? Chances are *Chasing Mavericks* will be yet another sub-par surf flick, but still – I'm going to reserve judgement until I've seen it for myself.

Songs for surfboards: a win-win exchange on Lewis

MIKE Guest is one of Scotland's most talented surf photographers, and also one of life's great collaborators – a man who likes to describe himself as 'a connector of people'. No great surprise, then, when he called me up to explain the concept of this exchange of ideas, goods and services on the Isle of Lewis, to which he was contributing still pictures and film. Sure, money makes the world go round, but cold, hard cash mostly removes the need for social interaction. The barter economy, by contrast, is all about building relationships, and that was exactly what was happening here, when Lewis-based musician and surfer Colin MacLeod suggested that, in exchange for some recording time in his Further North Music studio, English surfboard shaper and musician Will Brawn might be prepared to shape him a longboard. What Brawn hadn't bargained for, however, was a one-off stealth-recording mission to a local church. Also, as he suggests at the end of this piece, Guest did indeed turn this adventure into a short film called *Taking Shape*, a beautiful, low-key record of the whole interaction which premiered at the London Surf Film Festival.

18 February 2015

The barter economy gets a bad press, but whether you think bartering is crude, outdated, hopelessly idealistic or all of the above, you have to admit that there's at least a fundamental honesty at its core that capitalism lacks. Jesus may have thrown the moneylenders out of the temple, but as far as I can recall he never kicked anybody's ass for swapping chickens for sheep or sheep for donkeys. I love a good barter as much as the next wannabe-urban-hippy-with-a-mortgage, so I was intrigued to learn the other week about a strictly cash-free exchange going on in the Outer Hebrides involving top Scottish musician and surfer Colin Macleod (aka The Boy Who Trapped The Sun) and

English surfer, surfboard shaper and aspiring troubadour Will Brawn. The pair met a couple of years ago while Brawn was on a surf trip to Lewis. Brawn, at that time a sponsored rider for NinePlus surfboards, was having an evening session at Barvas – a beautiful reefbreak that lies to the north-west of Stornoway. Macleod paddled out to join him, the pair got chatting in between sets and a friendship was forged.

Fast-forward to January this year, and Brawn was back on Lewis, this time to record his debut EP at Macleod's Further North Music studios. In return for making use of the recording facilities and Macleod's not inconsiderable skills at the mixing desk (he recently recorded Rachel Sermanni's upcoming album, *Tied to the Moon*), Brawn agreed to shape Macleod a surfboard. Not just any old surfboard either, but a classic, old-school longboard – 9ft 8in in length, and with a single, deep fin to facilitate the noble art of noseriding, whereby the surfer cross-steps his way balletically to the end of the board and perches there for as long as he can, rocketing along the wave face with nothing in front of him but water and air. 'I got in touch with Will pretty randomly,' says Macleod, 'I guess it was a pretty strange email – somebody you meet once in the middle of nowhere says "Hey, do you wanna come up and hang out for a week and make a board and record some songs?" But luckily enough he was up for it and it's been great – I'm really glad we did it. We've tried to be as flexible with it as possible, but we've mostly been outside surfing and shaping the board during the day and then coming inside in the evening, getting all the gear going and recording.'

One of the songs – *Hold Down* – was recorded in the resonant acoustics of Europie Church. 'That was a bit of a sneaky one,' confesses Macleod, 'we weren't really supposed to be there, but that's cool, they probably all know anyway – you can't keep anything a secret on Lewis.' The 'two-takes-and-run-away' approach to recording might not suit everyone, but somehow Brawn manages to sound entirely relaxed and unhurried. Lyrically, the song seems to be about a surfer trying to relax as he is pinned underwater by the force of a breaking wave, but Brawn insists it's open to interpretation: 'It's an analogy, that one – an analogy for life.'

The EP, Brawn's debut recording, is a mixture of instrumental and vocal material, and he hopes to release it in the autumn. 'I've been working on music for a few years now,' he says, 'and creatively for me this was a really good time to start putting some things down, so I jumped at the opportunity.'

And how's the surfing been? 'We've had a couple of epic sessions,' he says. 'The first session was a little bit overhead on a reef – very clean, sunny . . . well, sunny with intermittent snow . . . and then we had another session at a little left-hander, with smaller, longboard conditions – amazing surf.' Edinburgh-based filmmaker Mike Guest has been on hand to document the project, and is hoping to turn it into something for the London Surf Film Festival in October.

He had to turn down other (paid) work to see the project through, but he reckons it has been worth it. 'It just felt like one of those things that you have to go into 100 per cent,' he says. 'It's been great. I've had so much fun.'

David C Flanagan's Orcadian surf Odyssey

I WAS once accused on social media of being monumentally ignorant, or words to that effect, by an Australian academic who took exception to my suggestion that surfing hadn't produced a body of literature of equivalent size or standing to that of, say, mountaineering. Clearly, then, there are a lot of books out there about surfing that I have yet to read, many of them no doubt Australian, and you should take the first few paragraphs of this next story with a pinch of salt. However, based on my experience of the UK publishing industry (and as arts and books editor at *The Scotsman*, that includes many years of receiving a waist-high sack full of books in the post every morning) books about surfing are generally few and far between. All of which made the arrival of David C Flanagan's 2015 memoir *Board* a bit of an event. Not just a book about surfing, but a book about surfing in Scotland. Even the Aussie academic would have to concede that there haven't been many of those.

23 March 2015

Until a few years ago, surfing had produced surprisingly little in the way of notable literature. I say surprisingly, not because surfers are a particularly literary tribe, but because surfing is just the kind of man-against-nature endeavour that great, existential yarns are made of. By the turn of the millennium, climbing, sailing and even fishing had all generated notable tomes, but surfing was still waiting for its *Touching the Void*, its *Sailing Alone Around the World* or its *Old Man and the Sea*. Things began to look up in 1999, when the American journalist Dan Duane published *Caught Inside*, his memoir of a year spent surfing along the California coast. Thoughtful and lyrical, it redefined what a surfing book could be, focusing as much on the natural and cultural history of this iconic surf zone as on the act of surfing itself. Keeping up the British end, in 2007, was Alex Wade's excellent *Surf Nation* – a journey through the esoteric surf culture of the UK that came across a little like Bill Bryson's *Notes From A Small*

Island, only with grinding, frigid, dark brown barrels lighting up the shorelines of otherwise tired, neglected seaside towns.

And then, in 2008, the Australian writer Tim Winton gave us what was arguably the first truly great work of surfing literature: his intoxicating, multi-award-winning novel *Breath*, in which two teenage boys in smalltown Western Australia, Pikelet and Loonie, come of age while pushing each other into waves of ever greater consequence, egged on by a former professional surfer named Sando. *Breath* was even made Radio Four's Book at Bedtime, and so middle-aged, middle-class audiences were able to swoon themselves to sleep while listening to such mellifluous lines as 'I came home at dusk with my ears ringing from the quiet'.

There have been other notable additions to the canon of serious surf lit in recent years – honourable mentions should go to Andy Martin for *Stealing the Wave* (2008), his account of the fearsome rivalry between big wave chargers Ken Bradshaw and Mark Foo; and to Tom Anderson for *Riding the Magic Carpet* (2006), in which the author describes how he spent several years (not to mention thousands of pounds) getting himself physically and mentally ready to tackle the legendary pointbreak waves of Jeffrey's Bay in South Africa.

The market for surfing books is still by no means saturated, but anyone entering this arena today had better have a novel story to tell and a novel way of telling it. Which brings us to Orkney-based journalist David C Flanagan, whose new book *Board* has just been published by Edinburgh's Fledgling Press. Happily, Flanagan's memoir offers a surf story that's original on two levels: firstly, it puts an unexpected spin on the man-deals-with-mid-life-crisis-by-learning-to-surf cliché by having its protagonist getting to grips with the sport of kings in some of the most inhospitable conditions imaginable, namely the board-snapping, bone-crunching reefs of Orkney's Bay of Skaill; and secondly, it also details the author's parallel attempts to rekindle his childhood love of skateboarding – a passion which came to a sudden end one Sunday morning in Leith when he accidentally ploughed through a column of veterans attending a Remembrance Day service.

While experienced surfers may find themselves wondering why Flanagan didn't simply look for a nice beachbreak to learn on (at one point in the book he does exactly that, and suddenly starts to find life much easier) it's impossible not to admire his sheer, bloody-minded determination, paddling out into the North Atlantic week after week, year after year, only to be pummelled by ten-foot walls of water and washed back to the beach with his confidence in tatters. His honesty, too, is admirable, both when describing the fear he feels when things go wrong and when analysing his reasons for trying to accomplish something that most people seem to think is nuts. And when he finally finds himself skimming across the open face of a wave at Skaill, following various injuries, near-death-experiences and long, dark nights of the soul, and is reduced 'almost to tears' by the experience – well, you'd have to be a hard-hearted reader not to find yourself welling up a little too.

When Charles Dance starred in a Scottish surf flick

FUN fact: Charles Dance did the voiceover work on 2016 Scottish surf flick *Edges of Sanity*. Yes, that Charles Dance, *the* Charles Dance, yer actual Charles Dance, Charles Dance OBE, Raymond, Lord Stockbridge in *Gosford Park*, Lord Kitchener in *The King's Man*, Tywin Lannister in *Game of Thrones*, Lord Mountbatten in *The Crown*. That guy. And the best thing of all? The film's director Chris McLean offering to pay him in surfing lessons – an offer he politely declined, but, who knows, perhaps politely but also with a raised eyebrow and just a hint of Lannister menace.

16 May 2016

Eighteen months ago, the award-winning British filmmaker Chris McClean brought out a surfing short called *Edges of Sanity*, under the aegis of UK surf brand Finisterre. The film was remarkable for all kinds of reasons, not least the stylish, committed surfing of Noah Lane and Matt Smith in shallow, slabby waves, and the potent combination of McClean's moody cinematography and the brooding CJ Mirra soundtrack, which conspired to make the north of Scotland look and feel like the end of the earth. What really made *Edges of Sanity* stand out from the thousands of other surf flicks doing the rounds online, however, was the poem intoned over the action, written by Dan Crockett.

The spoken word rarely features in surf films, which often just consist of visuals and music, and when it does it's usually the kind of jaunty, slightly tongue-in-cheek narration for which Bruce Brown established the template in the 1960s with films like *The Endless Summer*; to describe a surf flick/poetry combo as something of a novelty, then, is to understate the case. And what about the voice of the guy reading the poem? Gravelly, full of foreboding and also strangely familiar. Sounds a bit like Charles Dance. Hang on a minute, it is Charles Dance. 'He's not a surfer unfortunately,' chuckles McClean, 'we tried to pay him in surf lessons but he wasn't having any of it.'

'Finisterre's marketing director at the time [Ernie Capbert] said to me "Who do you want to read the poem?"' McClean continues, 'so I went away and thought about it and happened to come across a recording of Charles Dance reading something. I said "This would be perfect" – kind of jokingly. But then Ernie asked around, found his agent, emailed him and said "Look, we've not got very much money but we've got a cool project, would you like to be involved?" And he said yes. 'A few weeks later we were in the studio with him, which was quite surreal. From the very first take he did, the hairs on everyone's necks just stood up.'

On Friday, McClean will visit An Lanntair on Stornoway to present *Chasing Zero* – a 40-minute 'greatest hits' screening of his short surf films, with a live soundtrack performed by regular contributor Mirra. Some of McClean's films feature footage of surfing on Lewis, and there will also be surf films by locals including Mark Lumsden, Colin Macleod and Jim Hope, in what's being billed as a night 'celebrating the surf culture of the Outer Hebrides'. McClean hails from Cleethorpes in Yorkshire and grew up surfing around Scarborough, but his dark, moody take on surf cinematography is equally well-suited to capturing waveriding in austere, windswept Scottish settings. 'Surfing on the east coast isn't beautiful,' he says, 'it is dark and it does rain and, y'know, it's quite a bleak landscape in a lot of ways. It's just my take on surfing, I guess.'

There's something stylishly understated, too, about the way McClean presents the act of surfing. Surf films typically make a big deal of any star surfers they feature, but even when McClean's films show mind-blowing moves from global surf stars like Hawaii's John John Florence, you don't find out about their involvement until the end credits. Aesthetics take precedence over reputation. Unsurprisingly perhaps, McClean cites the groundbreaking 1996 surf film *Litmus* as a key influence. At a time when the mainstream surf media was still predominantly interested in world tour surfers cutting loose in tropical locations, Andrew Kidman's film made a point of profiling idiosyncratic elder statesmen like Tom Curren, Derek Hynd and Wayne Lynch. It wasn't afraid of the dark, either, frequently slipping into monochrome, or indeed the cold, showing Joel Fitzgerald surfing frigid, gurgling barrels in Ireland. The other key thing about *Litmus* was that it was the result of a multidisciplinary collaboration, featuring a soundtrack by the Val Dusty Experiment – a musical collective in which Kidman played a part – and animation by Mark Sutherland. It's a way of working McClean appreciates: 'Of course you can make a film on your own, but if you can't do everything you can assemble a really cool crew, and if you've got people like CJ and Dan you end up with a higher quality end product. From the very first film, that was always really exciting for me.'

Scottish surf journalism, 1970s style

IN THE unlikely event that anyone ever gets round to creating a museum of Scottish surfing, one of the star exhibits would have to be a complete collection of *Point Break*, the official magazine of the Edinburgh Surf Club. The copy gifted to me by Scottish surfing pioneer Andy Bennetts, dating back to 1975, is a real time capsule – and in the pre-internet days of its publication, when it would have been the only place for surfers in the south-east of Scotland to read about surfing in the south-east of Scotland, you can imagine it would have had a small but extremely devoted readership.

26 October 2017

Let's journey back to the days when Scottish surfing was still in its infancy via a couple of fascinating artefacts that now seem like relics of some ancient civilisation. The other day, Andy Bennetts – who is the nearest thing Scottish surfing has to an official historian – handed me a copy of *Point Break*, the Edinburgh Surf Club Magazine, dating from 1975 (Volume 1, Issue 3, cover price 10p) and a copy of the programme for the 1993 European Surfing Championships, which were held in Scotland that year, in the waves around Thurso.

Produced using nothing more sophisticated than a typewriter, a photocopier and a staple gun, *Point Break* was evidently a real labour of love. On the cover there's a line-drawing of the right-hander at Pease Bay breaking with typical ruler-edged precision, with a sea of static caravans in the foreground and a couple of figures down by the shore who may or may not be surfers checking out the waves. In his introduction on page three, the magazine's newly appointed editor Robin Salomon explains that, having taken over the role from Bennetts so that he could put more energy into running other aspects of the surf club, he will be aiming to make *Point Break* a bi-monthly publication and 'a real threat to *Surfer*'. He also explains that 'all complaints about typing and spelling mistakes will be treated in strict confidence and then disregarded.'

The mag is full of unexpected insights into what life was like for Scotland's first generation of wave-riders. It's well-known, for example, that there was a big audience for informal surf film screenings in California in the 1960s and 70s, but who would have thought that a screening of Jim Freeman and Greg MacGillivray's 1972 classic *Five Summer Stories* would have drawn a crowd of 120 at Leith Town Hall? The Edinburgh Surf Club apparently feared the event might be 'an expensive wash-out' but in the end they 'only lost a couple of quid'.

Another period highlight is Part Three of a guide to building your own surfboard. These days the complicated and messy art of surfboard manufacture is not something most surfers tend to get involved with, but 40-plus years ago, when ready-made boards were expensive and hard to come by, there was apparently quite a DIY scene. Other highlights include a report from the 1974 Scottish National Championships, which saw Batten narrowly beating Bennetts and Salomon in two-to-four foot surf at Pease Bay; a guide to surfing at Machrihanish on the Mull of Kintyre ('low-flying golf balls can be dangerous to the unwary'); and an anonymous dispatch from 'The Voice of the North' telling adventurous East Coast surfers about some of the gems to be found in and around Thurso.

The Eurosurf 93 programme is also very much of its time, although in this case it's really the adverts that date it: the back page ad for Gul wetsuits, for example, has English surfer Russell Winter sporting a day-glo Gul G-Force suit that's so bright it makes your teeth hurt, while the ad for *Wavelength* magazine on page four shows Aussie Tom Carroll in his musclebound, power-surfing prime. The last few pages are left blank with the word 'results' at the top, presumably so that spectators can keep their own record of the action.

Now, of course, things are a bit more hi-tech. As I write this, Eurosurf 2017 is in full swing over in Jæren, Norway, and I've been watching it live online. Rather than scribbling notes in the back of my programme, if I want to find out how Team Scotland are doing I need only click on the 'results' button on the Eurosurf website and I can see that, while most of the team have now been eliminated, Phoebe Strachan is still going strong in the women's bodyboard category and Joel Christopherson is still in with a shout in the men's bodyboard. All of which is very convenient, of course, but no amount of computer code could ever replicate the romance of a young surf mag editor feeding a fresh sheet of paper into his typewriter, cracking his knuckles, and then hammering out the first few lines of a brand new issue.

Laura Maynard on capturing Lewis's surf community on canvas

LAURA Maynard's striking portrait paintings of Lewis surfers, shown at An Lanntair in Stornoway in 2019 in an exhibition called *Wave Migration*, are full of little details that speak to the unique identities of their subjects. Taken together, they also capture a real sense of community – of a group of people from all walks of life and from all over the UK, drawn together by their shared love of the sport. One member of this community was Mark Lumsden, originally from Berwick-upon-Tweed, who first travelled to Lewis to make his era-defining 2001 surf film *Cold Rush* and then moved to the island full-time, working as a mechanic, shaping surfboards and surfing the cobblestone reef at Barvas whenever he could. It was while surfing at Barvas, in the autumn of 2019, that he tragically lost his life at the age of 48. Derek Macleod, of the local surf school Hebridean Surf, described him as 'a lovely, happy guy with an infectious laugh, the nicest guy I think I have ever met.'

Three of Lumsden's surfboards were included in the *Wave Migration* show. In the activity packs given out to children visiting the exhibition, one of the exercises was as follows: 'Can you see the surfboards on the wall? They are made by a surfboard shaper and designer called Mark who lives nearby, in Ness. Mark has made these especially for surfing here in the Hebrides. Can you see that they are each slightly different in shape? They have different noses and tails and thickness. Each suits different waves and different weather and each one is different to suit the surfer too. In the space below you can design your own surfboard – will you make yours skinny and long or short and curvy? What about the colours and design – can you choose a few of your own personal symbols to decorate it?' Perhaps, then, as well as leaving us an iconic surf film, Lumsden might also have inspired the next generation of Hebridean surfboard shapers.

4 April 2019

Opening on Saturday at An Lanntair arts centre in Stornoway and running until 11 May, *Wave Migration* is an exhibition of large-scale portraits by Lewis-based artist Laura Maynard, featuring members of the local surfing community. Usually when you see the word 'migration' used in reference to the Western Isles, you can be fairly certain that you're about to read something to do with population decline – a 2014 study predicted that the population of the Outer Hebrides as a whole will fall 13.7 per cent by 2039, and headlines about the islands' shrinking population crop up periodically in the pages of the *The Stornoway Gazette*. However, if there's one cast-iron good news story to be found in the delicately balanced demographic profile of the region, it's that of Lewis's surfing community, which has been growing steadily since the 1990s. Many of Maynard's subjects, she says, are people who have decided to move to Lewis from the mainland primarily so they can enjoy its solid, reliable, year-round waves.

'Most of my friends are people who have moved to the island,' she says, 'and I love that injection of people with new ideas from different places, and the community that it's made.' Maynard considers herself to be living through a golden age for surfing on Lewis, with a small, tight-knit community of like-minded souls who 'all get on really well together' but none of the out-of-control crowds that plague similarly wave-rich zones elsewhere in the world. The idea for her *Wave Migration* project – a series of 15 portraits, each one depicting a different Lewis surfer alongside their favourite surf break on the island – grew in part out of a desire to 'document this golden age, this little point in time.'

The portraits also contain subtle clues about the surfers' lives – what they do and where they come from. Her painting of her husband Kev, for example, pictures him alongside his favourite wave, Barvas, which breaks on a beautiful cobblestone beach on the west coast of the island, but it also hints at the journey that brought him there: the industrial landscape of his native Hartlepool also features in the image, as do a few subtly-placed magpie feathers – a nod to his love of Newcastle United. 'He'd been coming up here for years, I think since the late 90s,' says Maynard. 'He'd found it in the days when you used to look at Ceefax or Teletext to check the waves. He said he kept noticing this place and it kept saying 6–8 foot and clean, 6–8 foot and clean, and he kept saying "Wow, this place is amazing all the time, I'm going to go there." So he got in his van – all his pals were going to Ireland and Cornwall but he said "Nah, I'm off" – and he found this little gem.'

Another surfer, PJ, is pictured beside a thick-lipped barrelling wave and a synoptic chart. 'That's because he works for the Met Office,' Maynard explains, 'he's a weatherman. He's the guy you phone and go "Pete, what's the swell doing? What's happening?

What's it going to be like?" The chart is based on the swell conditions that you would need for his favourite break. It's a secret spot that one, so I can't name it!' On Lewis, as in many remote but surf-rich locations, the locals tread a fine line between welcoming outsiders and trying to keep their best waves from becoming too crowded. 'The surfers here are so down to earth, so friendly,' says Maynard, 'there's almost a non-scene if you see what I mean. They love people coming and finding out about the waves, but I don't think anyone really wants to broadcast it either – which has always been a bit of a rankle with me about doing the exhibition, because on the one hand I love the stories and I love the people, but also I might be part of the thing that could break what I love. It's a real conflict I think.'

In addition to Maynard's paintings, the *Wave Migration* show will also feature a short film about Lewis's surf culture by local surfer, photographer and filmmaker Jim Hope and three surfboards crafted by local shaper Mark Lumsden. 'Mark's another one that travelled all over the world and went on the most epic surf trips before ending up here,' says Maynard. 'He's got this lovely little cottage up in Ness and he's transformed the shed into a shaping bay. The three boards in the exhibition have all been made for local surfers, and he believes in making a board for the type of wave or the break you're going to surf.'

Maynard grew up on Lewis before studying fine art at Duncan of Jordanstone in Dundee. She now works as an art teacher at the Nicholson Institute in Stornoway, teaching S1 to S6. She recently went down to four days a week so that she could devote more time to her own work. 'I kind of fell into portraiture as a way of doing this project, because I loved the stories,' she says, 'but I don't think I'll continue doing portraits in future. I can't imagine doing anything other than something related to the sea though. I just can't seem to get away from it. Every time I try and do something else I always seem to end up coming back to something to do with waves or water.'

Dawn Days: riding out the
pandemic one sunrise at a time

DURING the Covid-19 pandemic, people in the surfing world found all kinds of different ways of dealing with the restrictions of lockdown. Famously, at the usually wildly overcrowded Malibu Beach in California, a lone surfer happily accepted arrest after taking the opportunity to get the place all to himself for a while. For Scottish surf photographer Mike Guest, meanwhile, lockdown solace came in the form of a meditative video project called *Dawn Days*.

6 June 2020

Lockdown has affected different people in different ways, but it has perhaps been hardest for those living alone. Parents juggling full-time jobs and homeschooling duties may scoff, but being stuck in the same place for days on end with only very limited human interaction can take its toll on even the most self-reliant souls. Add a bit of heartache to the mix and – without the possibility of therapeutic physical contact with friends and family – it's easy to see how things could get pretty dark, pretty quickly.

This was the position Edinburgh-based surfer and surf photographer and filmmaker Mike Guest found himself in towards the end of March, when, having just split-up with his long-term partner and been forced to abandon an exciting, globe-trotting project with innovative outdoors brand Patagonia, he found himself back in his Portobello flat with way too much time on his hands. 'I moved back into the flat and I just sat on the floor and my world was spinning,' he says. 'I just sat there thinking "Fuck, I've not spent time on my own for 21 years. I've just kept moving – and I've been happy, but ultimately I've never learned how to live with myself, how to sit with myself and deal with my thoughts."'

Help, however, came in an unlikely form. 'At the end of April I was on a phone call to another photographer, Nick Pumphrey – we know each other through the whole surf network. At the end of the call he said "Do you know what? I think I'm going to swim out [to sea] every day of May, at dawn, at the blue hour, and shoot until the sun comes up." I was like: "That's pretty cool, I might join you – you're gonna do it in Cornwall, I'm gonna do it in Scotland." And that was it.'

In Edinburgh at this time of year, getting up at dawn means getting up early – a whole hour earlier than in Cornwall. At the start of May Guest was getting up at 4.15am; then he realised that nautical first light is even earlier than first light on land, so by the middle of the month 3.30am starts were the norm. 'When I went down on the first morning I was just going to take photos because I really wanted to work on my abstract water photography,' he remembers. 'But then I was bobbing around and I started thinking, "I've got this amazing camera, and video-wise I want to understand it more," so I started shooting video too.'

When he got home, Guest edited together some of the images he'd captured, 'put a bit of music over it, a bit of ambiance' and then posted the resulting film on his social media channels. He called the project *Dawn Days*. The response was dramatic: hundreds of likes on Instagram, and dozens of positive comments, with people locked down in cities with no way of accessing big horizons telling him his films were keeping them going. As the days passed, the films became more ambitious, and then musical collaborators started getting involved.

'I started by just pulling free music off the internet,' says Guest, 'but then my friend Barry Jackson, a sound engineer who lives nearby, gave me this half-finished album and said "go for it". Then he started making me loops on synthesizers – just really mellow, calm tones. He would come back from work [at the BBC in Glasgow] and he would start making stuff for me. He would start vibing off the video from the day before, and more often than not, his vibe would match the weather, and it would match the way I was feeling – it was weird.'

Other musicians got involved too, notably Colin Macleod and Julie Fowlis. 'I cheekily tagged Julie Fowlis on one of my posts,' says Guest. 'I love Julie's music, her voice is amazing, I don't speak Gaelic but there's a lot of Gaelic stuff about Selkies and she was totally into it. She said, "OK, I'll have a think," and then she came back with this track. I listened to it obsessively that day and then I went down to the beach past Joppa to this bell tower. I was sat at the edge of the water, and I was listening to this tune and I just broke into tears. I was so affected by that music and all the other stuff I'd been dealing with. Then I went out and filmed with a lens combination I probably shouldn't have, but it meant I had to concentrate, I had to really relax and hold my posture right and just focus . . . and ultimately that's what this has turned into – a mental health project.' Even though May is now over, Guest is planning to keep his dawn filming sessions going at least once a week. 'I'm really lucky – that's something that I mustn't ever forget, I'm really lucky to be able to just walk down the road and do this. Because there are a lot of people who can't.'

The art of letting go: how to
parent a teenage big wave surfer

OSTENSIBLY, Martyn Robertson's film *Ride the Wave* is a documentary about the coming-of-age of Tiree big wave surfer Ben Larg. Charting his progress from promising but dissatisfied contest surfer to ecstatic conqueror of super-sized walls of water, it marks not just a watershed moment in the early life of its subject, but also a watershed moment in the history of Scottish surfing. In 2010, when I interviewed Chris Noble at Thurso East after he became the first Scot to make it through the first round of a pro contest, he said he thought Scotland might produce a full-time pro surfer one day. Ten years on, this film effectively captures the moment when that possibility became a reality. Not long after *Ride the Wave* was released, Larg signed a sponsorship deal with extreme sports behemoth Red Bull, and now officially gets paid to ride waves for a living. However, the film isn't just about Larg – it's also about his parents, Marti and Iona. If parenthood is all about learning to let go, about trusting your children to take ever greater risks, then *Ride the Wave* is about as stark and visceral an exploration of that process as you'll see anywhere.

16 October 2021

Premiering this weekend at the London Film Festival, *Ride the Wave* is a Scottish-made documentary about Ben Larg, a teenage surfer from the idyllic Hebridean island of Tiree who travels around the world to compete in similarly idyllic locations in Portugal and Japan. It might sound like an undemanding watch, but don't be fooled: it's anything but. Early on, we learn that Ben is being bullied at school, and we're not just talking about other kids calling him names. In a heart-wrenching scene, his mum, Iona, describes one particular incident that left the whole family reeling.

This violent episode provides the catalyst for the film's key moment: Iona and her husband Marti's decision to take Ben, 14, and his two younger sisters out of school and travel to Ireland, so that Ben can follow his dream of surfing giant waves at legendary breaks like Aileen's in County Clare and Mullaghmore Head in County Sligo. Just to be clear: these are places that most experienced surfers will a) discuss in hushed tones and b) never, ever want to surf. When the swell gets big at these spots, the potential for serious injury and death is very real, and director Martyn Robertson does an intelligent job of highlighting the dangers without sensationalising them. Partly he does this through his use of breathtaking slow-motion footage that emphasises the overwhelming size and power of the waves, but he also makes good use of a conversation between Ben, Marti and Iona and Irish big wave safety expert Peter Conroy, who offers to take Ben under his wing and teach him the finer points of big wave surfing, including how to catch waves while being towed behind a jetski.

By way of preparation, Conroy shows the Largs video footage of Ireland's big wave spots at their most terrifying, and he also shows them some horrific injuries and harrowing rescues. 'This is what you don't want to see,' he says, as something resembling a butcher's shop appears on the TV screen they're all looking at, 'an open femur fracture.' He then goes on to describe how the injured surfer in this case initially thought there was someone bobbing in the water beside him after being hit by a wave, before he realised that he was actually kicking himself in the back of the head with the floppy, disjointed remains of his own smashed-up limb.

Following their conversation with Conroy, then, the Largs are under no illusions about what the consequences of surfing these spots might be for Ben. Yet, as a counterbalance to the stark realities laid out by Conroy, there's another local surfer, Ollie O'Flaherty, a mellow, open-hearted soul who spends time hanging out with Ben and chatting to him about what surfing big waves means to him. 'You can spend so much time ruminating,' he says, 'lying in bed, looking up at the ceiling and imagining . . . if I got washed in here, or if I wiped out there . . . if this happened, if that happened . . . but all those things just stop when you're on the wave, and in the moment completely. If anybody catches a wave like that, they don't just do it once, they'll want to do it over and over again.'

To properly understand how Larg ended up talking big wave philosophy with O'Flaherty, though, sitting high up on the Cliffs of Moher overlooking the reef at Aileens, we first need to rewind a little to the initial third of the film, which shows Larg representing Scotland at various international contests in much smaller surf. He may have won the Scottish Under-18s title at the tender age of 12, but like countless talented surfers before him Larg seems to find the constraints and pressures of having to perform to order in timed heats perpetually frustrating. In a sense, then, his desire to surf big waves is as much about looking for new ways to express himself in the water as it is about processing troubles back home.

And Robertson takes us even further back in time, too, to a story Ben wrote when he was in primary school, in which he is running through a forest with his surfboard under his arm, pursued by a dark shadow. The shadow tells him he's going to die, but he goes surfing anyway. 'I realised I really shouldn't be in the water,' he writes, 'then I saw a huge wave . . .' Robertson's film is excellent at teasing out all the different things driving Ben towards his date with destiny at Mullaghmore – the desire to prove himself, the need to evolve as a surfer, his deep-seated fascination with giant waves. Its greatest achievement, though, is the way it also manages to be a film about parenthood: Ben may be at the centre of the film, but any parents watching will surely identify with Marti and Iona as they try to strike the right balance between protecting their son and allowing him to follow his dreams. It's a universal dilemma, of course, but few will have to deal with it on such an epic scale.

'Saltwater fairytale' a notable addition to the canon of Scottish surf lit

THE fictional Aberdeenshire fishing town of Norhaven in Mark Jackson and James T Duthie's surfing novella *Sans Peur* is so vividly described that I can still picture it clearly, and several of the main characters still live rent-free in my head. Could it form the basis for a film one day? Absolutely. The most important job for the casting director? Picking the right actors to play the two elderly gents who spend their days down by the pier, offering wry, witty commentary on the action.

26 February 2022

Eleven years ago, writing in *The Surfer's Path* magazine, the journalist and author Alex Wade set out to answer two questions: 'Is there such a thing as "surf lit"? And if there is, is it any good?' In his introduction, he lamented the fact that, on the surface at least, 'surfing seems to stand alone among the mainstream adrenaline sports in not having produced a discernible literary tradition'. And he also wondered whether 'surfing's image of beach-brained vacuity and endless hedonistic summers deters writers from tackling the subject'. As he worked his way through a modestly-sized 'to read' pile, however, Wade discovered that there were indeed some surf scribes worth reading, ranging from Mark Twain, Herman Melville and Jack London in the early days, to Tom Wolfe in the 1960s, Kem Nunn in the 1980s, Dan Duane in the 1990s and Tim Winton in the 2000s. Surfing's literary tradition, he concluded, was 'sparse, but notable'.

Given that the entire surfing world has produced relatively little in the way of reading matter, then, it should come as no surprise that Scottish surf lit is particularly thin on the ground, Scotland, after all, occupying a position in the sport of surfing of roughly equivalent importance to Hawaii's place in the sport of curling. Still, if you're prepared to look hard enough, and you're not too fussy about Scotland playing a bit-part in a larger narrative, there's more writing about Scottish wave-riding out there than you might think.

Chris Nelson provides a good potted history of Scottish surfing in a chapter of his 2010 book *Cold Water Souls*, as does Roger Mansfield in his 2009 tome *The Surfing Tribe: A History of Surfing in Britain*. The second chapter of Tom Anderson's round-the-world surf odyssey *Riding the Magic Carpet* (2006) sees him searching for waves on Mainland Orkney and Westray before sampling a few roaring barrels at Thurso East, and Alex Wade concludes his own 2007 book *Surf Nation: In Search of the Fast Lefts and Hollow Rights of Britain and Ireland* with colourful tales of visits to Lewis, Orkney, Shetland and, of course, Thurso. Anyone looking for a pure, visceral hit of the Scottish surfing experience, meanwhile, would do well to get hold of a copy of David C Flanagan's 2015 book *Board*, in which the Orkney resident provides a refreshingly honest and ego-free account of what it was like learning to surf on the often lonely and frequently storm-thrashed reefs of the Bay of Skaill.

Beyond that, however, Scottish surf lit is tricky to find. At a push, we could perhaps include Kirsty Gunn's 2006 novella *The Boy and the Sea*, but although Gunn herself is based in Scotland, her story isn't. Either way, considering how few Scottish surf books are currently available, the recent publication of a new novella about two surfing fishermen from Aberdeenshire is a bit of an event.

Written by award-winning short film maker Mark Jackson and the late fisherman, playwright and political activist James T Duthie, *Sans Peur* appears in a collection of their work titled Norhaven, published by Troubador. The title is a reference to the fictional fishing town where *Sans Peur* and all the other stories in the collection are set – a place that might almost be Fraserburgh, were the Broch not mentioned as a nearby location in the text.

The Sutherland brothers, Alan and Graham, are the frequently warring duo at the centre of the action. Graham is the eldest, known to everyone as Suds, but although he has made the family name his own, in many ways Alan is the head of the clan: a better surfer than his brother, captain of their boat, the Sans Peur, while Suds is only a crewman, and married while Suds remains stubbornly single.

In fact, the Sans Peur is not really theirs at all: when their father died they inherited his fishing license, but his partner Peter took the boat for himself. Now a big noise in the local business community, Alan and Suds both work for Peter, and he seems determined to make their lives difficult at every turn – not least by making them work more and surf less. To make matters worse for Alan, he's married to Peter's daughter, Yvonne, so when the story begins his father-in-law seems to be holding most of the cards.

Sans Peur is billed as a 'saltwater fairytale', however, and the little bit of magic required to mix things up comes in the form of a group of travelling surfers from Ireland, who arrive in Norhaven just in time to compete in the local surfing contest. Among them is Abina, a surfer and folk singer who Alan finds strangely captivating, and her estranged partner Erin, who turns out to be Alan's main rival in the surf. As the two communities collide, sparks fly, much alcohol is consumed and two old gadgies sitting smoking on the pier act like a *Chewin' the Fat*-style Greek chorus. The text might have benefited from tighter editing in places, but the characters are so well-drawn and the plot so absorbing it doesn't really matter. A notable addition to the small but slowly growing canon of Scottish surf lit.

Fact or fiction? Decoding Malcolm Findlay's surf stories

For anyone with more than a passing interest in Scottish surfing, there was much fun to be had trying to decode the short stories in this book by Malcom Findlay, all of which, according to the author, have 'some connection to real events.' Which elements are real and which are imagined? The regular appearance of characters named after well-known Scottish surfers only added to the intrigue.

9 July 2022

You wait years for somebody to write a work of Scottish surf fiction and then two come along at once. Well, almost at once. Towards the end of last year, Troubador published a collection of writing by Mark Jackson and the late James T Duthie which included a surfing novella called *Sans Peur*. And now, none other than five-times Scottish National Surfing Champion Malcolm Findlay has released a book of surf-related short stories, which, while billed as fiction, certainly incorporate one or two names which will be familiar to those in the know.

Findlay could hardly be more of a surf world insider. Not only does he have those five Scottish titles under his belt, he has been involved in Scottish surfing right from the get-go, having first caught the bug back in the late 1960s, when most of the country's best surf spots were still waiting to be discovered. Having worked as a commercial fisherman until the 1980s, he then moved into academia, completing a doctorate on fishing vessel safety before establishing the world's first academic degree programme in surf science and technology at Plymouth University.

Titled *The Surfing Collection – Short Stories For and About Surfers*, Findlay's book is self-published via Amazon. It is definitely a work of fiction – the 'about the author' blurb states that 'while [Findlay] has published many scientific papers over the years, this is his first foray into fiction.' However, the blurb on the back also explains that 'all of the stories in this book have some connection to real-life events'. Given that the names of some of the characters will be familiar to many Scottish surfers, there's clearly a bit of fun to be had guessing which bits are based on real events and which are invented. For example, when Strachan, the hero of a story about a surf-by-boat adventure gone badly wrong, encounters another surfer called 'Scratch', should we infer that another Scottish surfing champion, Mark 'Scratch' Cameron, was once involved in a similar series of unfortunate events? Or is Findlay just imagining him into his tale? Similarly, when he gives three surfers who inadvertently consume industrial quantities of magic mushrooms the names 'Bennetts, Wishart and Batten', is he adapting a true story involving three of Scottish surfing's most revered pioneers, Andy Bennetts, Ian Wishart and Bill Batten? Or, again, is he just having fun imagining it?

Of course, it doesn't really matter either way – the tales here will entertain surfers and non-surfers alike, whether they are alert to the local references or not, and the characters and scenarios never feel less than true-to-life. Findlay is evidently not a graduate of a creative writing course – his style is functional rather than self-consciously literary. However, there's a lot to be said for substance over style, and these stories have plenty of substance to them. And for all that Findlay nails the minutiae of the surfing life, he is also alert to the bigger picture – stories like *Flotsam and Jetsam* and *Jelly Mountain* are intriguing meditations on the strange ways in which our lives can sometimes hinge on an apparently insignificant event or decision. In *Born to Surf*, meanwhile, he even dares to suggest that surfing might not be the be-all and end-all.

Ross Ryan on painting, sailing and surfing his way around Scotland

SURFING lore is full of boat-based adventures, from Martin Daly's decades-long exploration of the Mentawai Islands in Indonesia to the various high-profile attempts to ride giant waves at the Cortes Bank, a shallow seamount some 96 miles off the coast of California. There are fewer such voyages which also incorporate art into the mix, however, but that's exactly what Ross Ryan set out to do with his *Crinan to Catterline* project – a surfing and painting expedition taking in some of Scotland's most famous surf zones.

10 September 2022

Artist, sailor and surfer Ross Ryan is explaining the appeal of painting outside in the middle of a storm. 'It's about keeping it exciting,' he says. 'Being in a studio with a white canvas is really intense. It's all about your tea and your tunes – getting the AC/ DC on to get you fired up – but when you're outside it's all there in front of you and you can just get on with it.'

Showing at the Scottish Gallery in Edinburgh until 24 September, Ryan's latest exhibition, *Crinan to Catterline*, is a stunning visual record of a 1,300-mile voyage he made in his 40-foot fishing boat, Sgarbh, between May 2021 and March 2022. Along the way he visited Barra, St Kilda, Oldshoremore, Durness, Thurso, Wick and Peterhead, before heading home again via the Caledonian Canal. Ryan only ever paints outside, sometimes in the kind of storms which would have most people running for cover, and as a result the works in this exhibition aren't merely records of what he saw on his journey, but also records of the weather conditions he experienced. Paintings like *Squall, Iona, 27/1/22* and *Big, Bad Barra Blow, 8/2/22* feel kinetic in a way static images really have no right to, almost as if they've somehow absorbed some of the energy of the storms in which they were created.

'I think the adrenaline starts to kick in,' he says, of the challenge of working in gale force winds, 'and when you're down on the beach or the rocks or the boat and the weather's not great it becomes a bit like an operation, it needs military precision, it's like, "OK, if I don't put the lid on that it's going to blow away." Maybe it's a distraction from what you're about to do, but the process – I really love it. And you're sitting right in the face of nature . . . it's good – it helps keep you in your corner – it's these big, powerful elements and you're trying to record them.'

Ryan grew up in Crinan and graduated from Gray's School of Art in Aberdeen in 1997, and when he's not making art he runs charters on Sgarbh. He's an experienced surfer, too – although, as he puts it, 'more air than action these days' – and so this voyage around some of the best surf spots in the land was an opportunity to catch a few waves as well as to find fresh inspiration for his work. Before setting off, he ordered a brand new red surfboard, and even had the boat's logo glassed onto the deck. Of all the surf spots on his itinerary, he was most excited to try it out at the legendary right-hander at Thurso East, but – after a promising start to his first session there – things went badly wrong.

'I thought it would be nice to get a new board, just to give me some inspiration to get out there again,' he says. 'So I decided, right, I'm going to get a really special one this time. Anyway, the conditions were good, I was picking off some smaller ones on the shoulder, which is actually where it starts to barrel more. I had a couple of nice runs on the smaller ones, but then a big set came through – I went for it but I went right over the falls. When I came up the board was full of hairline fractures – I'd completely shattered the glass job, and I'd also broken my toe. So I came out and I was quite cross, but then I was like, "OK, it's just a board, now I'm going to go and paint this wave."'

The resulting painting, *Thurso East, Caithness, 11/1/22*, is a wonderful evocation of Scotland's most famous surf spot, perfectly capturing the way swells here fold over the reef, and also the way their power seems to be magnified as they reel along from right to left. Ryan also painted at nearby spot Bagpipes – an extremely shallow wave slamming down over almost-dry slabs of rock which is now on the international surf map, and is favoured by the kinds of professional freesurfers who prefer their waves on the hairy side. 'It's epic to watch, but I would never dream of surfing there,' he says. 'So yeah, to go down there when it's two or three metres and no surfers around, but you feel that you're doing your painting thing, you have the whole place to yourself . . . that's the new buzz!'

Ryan's final destination, Catterline, will always be synonymous with the artist Joan Eardley, and while he was there Ryan stayed in her former studio. His visit also coincided with some serious storms, and in the catalogue for the show he gives a vivid description of what painting there in these conditions was like. 'With all my layers on, I dragged out the largest board from the van,' he writes. 'Like grasping a pterodactyl by its wingtips, the huge board lurched frantically, crashing into the rocks in an effort to take flight. . . With the board secured, I laid out my tools, weighing down the palette with stones and selecting only the heaviest brushes.' It's a wonderful way to make art, but surely he can't keep it up forever, can he? Or can he? 'Hopefully I'll be able to paint until my last day,' he says, 'but I'm not going to be down on the beach when I'm an old man . . . well, maybe I am, but it won't be the same sort of thing – there would need to be carers everywhere . . .'

Bennetts and Findlay pen the definitive history of Scottish surfing

FOR anyone with an interest in the history of Scottish surfing, Malcolm Findlay and Andy Bennetts' book *Surfing Scotland* is essential reading. Because they were both involved from the very beginning of the 60s surf explosion – Findlay in Fraserburgh and Bennetts in south-east Scotland – and because they are both still surfing today, they are able to offer a uniquely authoritative overview of the last six decades.

6 November 2023

In attempting to write their new history of surfing in Scotland, Malcolm Findlay and Andy Bennetts set themselves a Herculean task. Most sports generate copious records – not just results and league tables, but also newspaper reports, interviews and more. Surfing, by contrast, is mostly practised for fun, rather than for points or prizes, and is all-but ignored by the mainstream media in the UK. So, while the main problem facing a historian looking to tell the story of Scottish football might be sifting through the mountain of available material and deciding what to leave out, for Findlay and Bennetts the biggest challenge will have been trying to fill in some of the blanks in a sketchy and threadbare narrative.

Fortunately, in writing *Surfing Scotland* the duo had the advantage of having been intimately involved in the Scottish surf scene from the early days. Originally from Edinburgh, Bennetts first caught the bug as a boy while on family holidays to Cornwall in the 1960s. In September 1968, having bought his first surfboard, he and two friends travelled to Aberdeen in search of waves, where they met Aberdonian George Law, who had been surfing there since 1967. This was the first recorded contact between two of Scotland's early surfing tribes. Findlay, meanwhile, started surfing in Fraserburgh in the 1970s and won the Men's Open division of the Scottish National Surfing Championships five times between 1977 and 1995 – an achievement notable not just for the number of wins, but also for the fact that they span almost two decades, during which time surfing technique and equipment changed significantly.

The authors begin with three brief introductory chapters: Scotland's Surf Geography, Climate and Weather; Scotland's

History; and The Body and Soul of the Scottish Surfer. As well as providing important background, these also set up their central thesis: that Scottish surfers are 'proudly different' from surfers in the rest of the UK, and that Scotland 'stands apart . . . from an increasingly homogenised global surf culture.' Such distinctions can be tricky to nail down but Findlay and Bennetts make a convincing case, referencing not just the harshness of Scotland's weather, but also the influence of its history and culture and the Scottish sense of humour.

Findlay and Bennetts then launch into the meat of their story with a chapter on 'The Early Days'. Even before Law started surfing in Aberdeen in '67, the Granite City already had an informal surf club. In 1965, *Boy's Own* magazine carried instructions on how to make a hollow wooden surfboard for £4 – Aberdonians Graeme Carnegie and Brian Morgan decided to get a couple built by a local joiner and these became the (leaky) surf vehicles of choice in the area until Morgan eventually bought a fibreglass board on a trip to Cornwall.

From here, the story is one of coalescence: small groups of surfers in Aberdeen, Edinburgh and Fraserburgh gradually became aware of each other, and a Scotland-wide surfing community began to take shape. This soon led to the formation of official surfing organisations, which are dealt with in the following chapter – first the short-lived Scottish Surf Club and then the Scottish Surfing Federation, which survives in good health to this day, not to mention various regional and university surf clubs. These organisations performed an important social function, bringing together like-minded souls committed to pursuing a minority sport. However, they also established competitions, the longest-running of which, the Scottish National Surfing Championships, has now been going for over 50 years.

The book's sixth chapter deals with competitive surfing – not just the Scottish Nationals, but also the various professional contests held in Scotland over the years as well as the Scottish national team's often colourful adventures on the international stage. There is also a chapter on Scotland's surf industry, taking in everything from surf schools to clothing brands, and a series of first-person accounts from present-day surfers living all around Scotland's coastline. Meanwhile the final chapter, The Future of Scottish Surfing, looks at the possible impacts of climate change, new technologies and demographic shifts.

Could there have been more on Scottish surfing culture? Perhaps, but then this is all fertile ground for Scotland's future surf historians. The great achievement of Findlay and Bennetts is to have set out, in a readable and accessible format, the main plot points of Scotland's surfing story. Others will no doubt add detail to the picture, but this seems destined to be the definitive book on the subject.

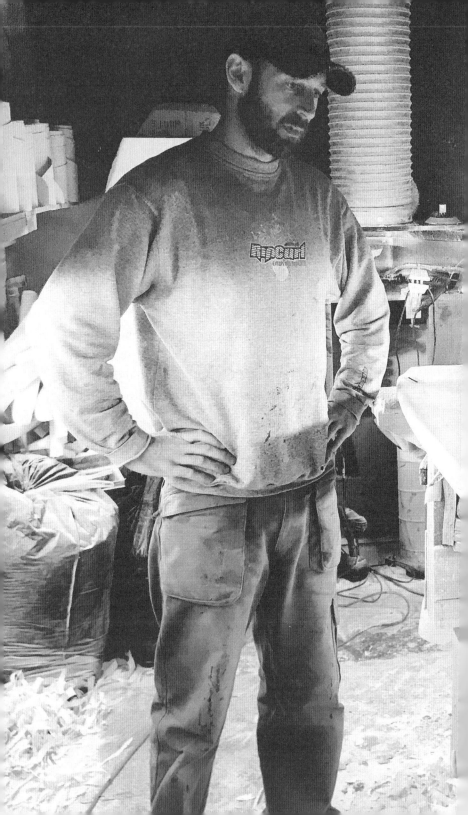

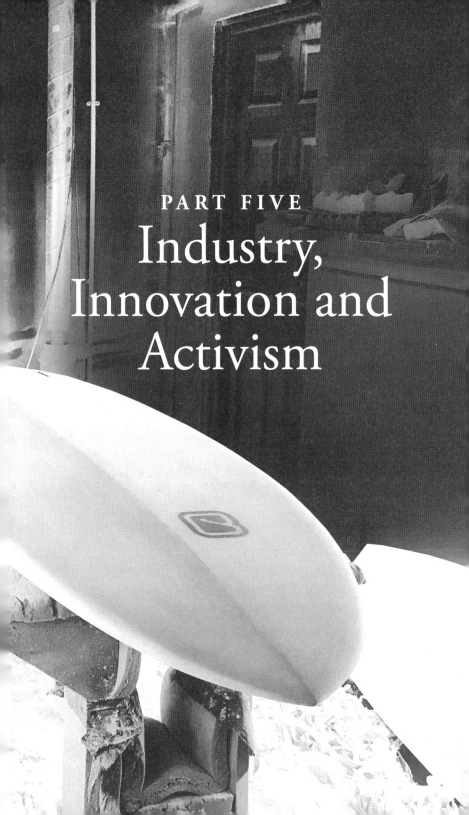

PART FIVE

Industry, Innovation and Activism

Previous pages: Surfboard shaper Jason Burnett working
on his latest creation, December 2017 (Janeanne Gilchrist)

'Waves nearly all the time' – happy days for Hebridean surf schools

IN GLOBAL terms, surfing is now a multi-billion dollar industry. In Scotland? Not so much. Still, there are those who make a living from the sport here, whether by offering lessons or selling equipment, and the last couple of decades have seen a marked growth in Scotland's surf infrastructure, from dedicated surf centres at Dunbar and Thurso to Lost Shore, the new £60 million artificial wave pool at Ratho. In an interview in 2024, Lost Shore founder Andy Hadden predicted that the advent of the wave pool would rapidly accelerate the growth of Scotland's surf industry, and it's hard to see how that won't happen. Back in 2006, though, only a handful of people seemed to be making a full-time living out of surfing and most of them were running surf schools. Two of these – Derek MacLeod and Craig Sutherland – were based in the Hebrides, where the supply of students tended to be limited and seasonal, but opportunities for finding good waves for their clients were endless.

22 April 2006

If there was such a thing as a World Understatement Championship, Derek MacLeod would win it every year. Since starting up Hebridean Surf Holidays in 1998, the former fisherman has ridden waves big enough to scare the living daylights out of most normal people – and most normal surfers – but he talks about his experiences in the same calm, measured way in which a mere mortal might discuss a recent trip to the supermarket. 'It gets quite big here,' he says, sipping from a mug of tea in the kitchen of the Sunset Restaurant in Stornoway – a business he runs in conjunction with the surf school. 'How big?' I ask. 'Too big. Too big for us.' 'Bigger than double overhead [12ft waves]?' 'Och, we're out in double overhead all the time. You get used to it after a while. Triple overhead is usual. It starts getting a bit hectic after that.'

A bit hectic? Clearly, going surfing out here can be a serious business. Unlike, say, Cornwall, where the continental shelf slopes gradually into the Atlantic, taking some of the sting out of incoming swells, the west coast of Lewis drops away steeply. On the right day, the two premier breaks on the island – Europie in the north and Barvas in the west – can hold world-class waves. You don't have to be an expert to surf on Lewis, however. 'There's a good variety of spots here, good beginner spots, bays that point north, bays that point south,' says MacLeod. 'And we put a lot of emphasis on safety – all our instructors are trained lifesavers now.'

Whatever your level of surfing experience, MacLeod and his team reckon to be able to find a spot to suit on any given day – swell permitting, of course. They also provide transport, boards, wetsuits, accommodation in Stornoway and meals if required.

Unless global warming really throws Scotland a curveball, Lewis will never become a crowded surf destination like Hawaii or California – for much of the year it's simply too dark and too cold. Even in the summer months, when it's possible to surf right through the night, MacLeod reckons that only a few hundred surfers visit the island.

That said, some of these visitors have been exceedingly distinguished. In September 2001 Lewis hosted the first International

Hebridean Surf Festival. Among the participants was three-time world champion Tom Curren – retired from the pro circuit, but still widely considered one of the greatest wave riders on the planet. MacLeod organised the festival with Australian Derek Hynd, former pro surfer, longtime surf journalist and one of the surfing world's most-revered elders. Some serious big-wave hunters have also travelled to Lewis, including Rusty Long of San Clemente, California – a contender for the £28,500 Billabong XXL prize for the biggest wave ridden in the winter of 2005/6. 'Rusty was here last year but he never got it,' says MacLeod. 'He was here for a few days and he got some double overhead stuff, but he never really got any big days.'

Lewis isn't the only place in the Hebrides where you can get a surf lesson. About 120 miles due south, Craig Sutherland (aka Suds) has established Wild Diamond Surf School on Tiree. The island is better known as a windsurfing destination, but west-facing beaches such as Balephuil and The Maze offer ideal surfing conditions. On the island's north-west tip there's also a stunning white sand beach called Balevullin – Sutherland's favourite spot for teaching beginners and also a good place to get barrelled when the conditions are right.

On a still-warm day in mid-October, the chirpy 28-year-old is busy teaching a mixed-ability group in small, pre-broken waves near the beach. Further out, a handful of locals and tourists are having fun in the dropping two-to-four-foot swell. 'It was fully barrelling here yesterday,' he says with a grin. 'You could hardly even make the drop on some waves, they were so steep. Normally the barrels here are easy enough, but yesterday you were just getting battered if you got it wrong. There were only about four folk out, I think.'

Sutherland initially moved to Tiree to work as a windsurfing instructor, but so many people approached him to ask where they could get surf lessons that he decided to start teaching them himself. Grants from Argyll and Islands Enterprise and the Prince's Scottish Youth Business Trust helped him buy all the wetsuits and soft surfboards he needed, and, after getting his instructor's qualifications in Cornwall in 2004, he hasn't looked back.

Tiree can be a desolate place in winter, and its waves go almost unsurfed for the colder half of the year. In the summer months, though, more and more people are making the pilgrimage from the mainland. 'This summer's been busy,' says Sutherland. 'We had a long season this year. The weather wasn't as good as it can be on Tiree, but there were still plenty of people to teach. Plus, we had waves nearly all the time, so it was great in that respect. We got a couple of flat spells here and there but they didn't usually last more than a few days, so it wasn't a problem. Most people are up for a week, so you'll at least get them in a handful of times.'

Like Lewis, Tiree is exposed to the open ocean and, in common with its northerly neighbour, it is sometimes pounded by monster surf. 'It gets huge here, but to be honest most of the beaches can only handle double overhead,' says Sutherland. 'Any bigger and you get all kinds of currents – you end up paddling forever. There are a few outer reefs, though. I think they have the potential for holding a lot bigger. There were a couple of guys who windsurfed one of them, but nobody's surfed them yet as far as I'm aware. I don't know how big they get but they've got to be pretty huge.'

In most places in the world, surfers tend to be very protective of their secret spots, but crowds aren't really a problem in the Hebrides. When asked about the location of these unridden reefs, Sutherland doesn't hesitate. 'There are a couple off Balaphetrish and a few off bays like Volem and Salem,' he says. 'They pick up quite a bit of swell, but the reefs up there don't tend to work right through the tides. They're just kind of rock ledges, so when the tide comes in it'll get too deep for them to work. You've got to time it.' Who knows? As you sit reading this, a couple of brave souls might already be paddling out to one of these giant open ocean breaks, checking their watches, weighing the odds.

The Newquay of the north? Attempts to tap Thurso's surf tourism potential

THREE years on from Russell Winter's dramatic win at the inaugural Highland Open at Brims Ness in 2006, by 2009 Thurso was getting used to being a regular stop on surfing's World Qualifying Series (WQS) – the feeder competition for the sport's top tier, then known as the World Championship Tour (WCT). With the increased exposure, however, came certain dilemmas. To what extent should the town be trying to capitalise on its new-found fame as a surfing destination? And how best to use the obvious appeal of its world class waves to boost the local economy? In the end, the proposed Harbour Centre building on the pier never came to fruition, but the idea was symptomatic of an ambitious moment.

8 May 2009

Kiwi surfer Rowan Aish is 'stoked'. He's just made it into the fourth round of the O'Neill Cold Water Classic event at Thurso, picking up US$2,000 in the process, and now he's standing at the water's edge, waxing lyrical about the waves on Scotland's north coast. 'There's a lot of potential here – world class potential,' he says. 'When the conditions are right, it's one of the best stops on the pro tour.'

However, Aish is a lot less enthusiastic about the prospect of competing at the UK's other big surf competition later this year, the Relentless Boardmasters in Newquay.

'I've been [there] twice now and it's probably the worst stop on tour for waves,' he says. 'It's sort of a party stop. A fun town, but the waves aren't great.' Newquay makes a fortune out of its status as 'Surf City UK', with road signs welcoming you to 'Europe's best surfing beaches'. Jo Hillman, Newquay-based operations manager at the British Surfing Association (BSA), estimates that surfing is worth £30–£40 million to the town each year. Its streets are lined with surf shops, its most popular breaks are permanently crowded with surfers and seven years ago a huge, £2.5 million National Surf Centre was built overlooking its premier break, Fistral Beach.

Here in Thurso there isn't really a surf industry at all – just one surf shop, the Tempest, down by the harbour. The sign visitors see when they approach from the west goes on to list the town's attractions: 'Accommodation, swimming pool, caravan site, walks, beach, museum' – but there's not a word about the surfing. For many years, after its potential was uncovered in the 1970s, Thurso was an open secret in the surfing world. Spectacular pictures of its perfect, powerful waves occasionally appeared in surf magazines, attracting the odd band of travelling wave-riders, but cold water and geographical isolation meant that a handful of local enthusiasts usually had the surf to themselves. All that changed in 2006, however, when the Association of Surfing Professionals (ASP) held a competition at two of the best breaks in the area: Thurso East and Brims Ness. The surf was so good that year that the event became a permanent fixture on the World Qualifying Series (WQS), the gruelling international round of competitions in which aspiring pro surfers must compete if they want to qualify for surfing's big bucks premier league, the World Championship Tour (WCT). Every year now, in late April and early May, between 120 and 150 of the best wave-riders on the planet descend on Thurso to do battle in the chilly waters of the Pentland Firth, and every year a big chunk of the world's surfing media travels with them, ensuring that pictures of huge, barrelling Scottish waves appear in surf magazines from Hawaii to Hamburg.

Thurso may have been slow to cash in on its new-found fame to begin with, but this year it seems to be making up for lost time. At the former Town Hall, now a stylishly converted visitor centre called Caithness Horizons, they're staging an exhibition of surfing memorabilia to coincide with the WQS contest. 'It made sense to do this at the same time as the international surfing competition is on,' says the centre's manager, Beki Pope. 'It raises its profile with people who wouldn't necessarily know the competition was happening. Today they're surfing out at Brims Ness, a couple of miles out of town, so there's no visibility in Thurso itself. But because we've got this exhibition here, people are thinking, "Oh, hang on a second, there are professional surfers up here and, oh look, our waves are quite good aren't they?"'

The thing that's really got the local surf community buzzing, though, is the prospect of a new surfing centre being built here. There are now well-advanced plans to construct a £700,000 watersports hub at the end of Thurso pier, featuring a large, first-floor observation deck which will offer spectators a grandstand view of the waves breaking at Thurso East. Designed by Pentarq Architects and funded by a newly established charity, Caithness Sports Facilities, the Harbour Centre, as it will be known, could become a reality in just a couple of years. 'We've got the support of the local council and there's detailed planning permission for it,' says Jim Kelly, director of Caithness Sports Facilities. 'We're looking at getting the funding together now, and all being well we'll have it finished by 2010 or 2011.'

The reaction from local surfers has been mixed. Andy Bain, of Caithness Boardriders Club, thinks the location is wrong. Although the new centre will be great for spectators, it's on the opposite side of the Thurso River from the surf spot, so he reckons surfers are unlikely to use its changing facilities. 'You really need something at Thurso East itself,' he says, 'because when people come to surf here, that's where they go. We're only a small surf club but we're working on putting something down there ourselves, even if it's just a little shack – just something that would get us out of the wind when we're getting changed. I can't see the new Harbour Centre being a building that we'd use a lot, to be honest. It's good what they're trying to do, but it's not going to benefit the surfing.' Chris Noble, president of the Scottish Surfing Federation, also has reservations about the proposed centre, particularly with regards to running costs. According to the latest proposal document, the local surf club – with a total membership of 25 – is expected to provide 32 per cent of these costs, or £2,840 a year. 'We'll just never be able to come up with the sort of money they're asking for,' he says, 'and I'm not sure if the kayakers and divers will be able to produce [it] either. What happens if none of us can [pay]? We'll just end up with a new building that nobody uses. Who does that benefit?' He can see advantages, too, however. 'It's helping to develop Thurso,' he says, 'and having somewhere for surfers to change is going to make it a bit more comfortable and civilised. It's certainly a fantastic idea.'

These are tricky times for Thurso's surfers. On the one hand, they love getting to watch the pros shred their waves once a year – the equivalent of having the football World Cup played out in your local park. Mark 'Scratch' Cameron, winner of this year's Scottish Surfing Championships, got the chance to compete against seasoned pros in the first round. But the publicity generated by the WQS competition has led to a marked increase in the number of travelling surfers who visit Thurso throughout the year. The waves aren't anywhere near as crowded as they are in Newquay, but initiatives like the proposed Harbour Centre can only result in more out-of-town surfers hitting the water.

To understand why this might be a problem, you only have to watch the pros surfing at Brims Ness or Thurso East. These are critical, hollow waves breaking in shallow water over sharp slabs of rock – wipeouts can result in serious injury. There's only room on the wave for one person at a time, but when a good one comes through, everybody wants it. Even in a professional heat, with just three or four surfers in the water, this can lead to tempers getting frayed – as when America's Matt Hohagen came to blows with Spain's Haritz Mendiluze during the first round of this year's WQS event. Put 20 surfers in the water at once – or 30, or 40 – and things could easily get out of control. 'Five years ago, there were maybe only two or three guys in the water every time we got waves,' says Noble, 'plus maybe a few travelling surfers. But now you have 10 guys regularly in the water, plus an increased number of travelling surfers. I guess the main problem is that waves are a limited commodity.'

The general consensus seems to be: develop surfing in Thurso, but proceed with caution. Beki Pope, for one, is well aware of the risks in over-promotion. 'We're trying to raise the profile [of surfing] a little bit,' she says, 'but obviously not too much. Everyone talks about overcrowding at the moment. Up here it's nothing like it is down south, but you still get some people muttering "Oh, there's too many people coming up here to surf".' Then again, there's also the feeling that the residents of Thurso are sitting on top of a potential gold mine. As the BSA's Jo Hillman puts it: 'They've got a much better asset [ie. waves] than we have in Newquay, but I guess they're just not as good at pushing it.'

Surfers Against Sewage: Policing Pease Bay's pathogens

MORE than a decade after this series of stories about the water quality at Pease Bay in the Scottish Borders appeared in print, the issue of sewage being released into Scotland's coastal waters is as pressing as it's ever been. In 2012, Surfers Against Sewage activists were primarily concerned with the fact that sewage released into the sea near Pease wasn't being treated to as high a standard in the autumn and winter as it was in the summer. In 2023, however, an investigation by the Ferret website revealed that a number of popular surf spots in south-east Scotland had exceeded safe sewage pollution limits during the summer of that year, not only Pease Bay but also Belhaven Bay and Coldingham. Surf spots elsewhere in Scotland where limits had been exceeded included Machrihanish in Argyll and Dunnet Bay in Caithness. The monitoring of these overflows is improving, however – see 'Safe to Surf' on p. 245.

28 October, 4 November and 11 November 2012

Back in 2009, *The Scotsman* reported that, at various sites around Scotland's coastline, sewage released into the sea was being treated to a lower standard in winter than in summer. During the so-called 'bathing season', from the start of June to the middle of September, the sewage at these sites is bombarded with UV rays before being released – a procedure that is said to reduce pathogen levels to around 35 particles per 100ml (a pathogen being any microorganism capable of causing disease in a host, for example, a human). For the rest of the year, however, the sewage receives what's known as secondary treatment, which only reduces pathogen levels to between 100,000 and 300,000 particles per 100ml. If you were going to drink a cupful of seawater from one of these locations for a dare, in other words, you'd be a whole lot better off doing it in July than in January. (Common pathogens in human sewage, by the by, include E coli, cryptosporidium, salmonella and campylobacter, all of which have the power to thoroughly mess up your weekend.)

Of course, if there's nobody in the water at these locations when the UV treatment has been switched off, there's nobody around to get ill, so none of this really matters. But what happens when you have a sewage outflow pipe located approximately 1,500m from a popular surfing beach – a beach that's used by several hundred surfers all year round?

Well, in the case of Pease Bay in the Borders, you get a lot of upset surfers who claim the water is making them ill.

Alasdair Steele is the Edinburgh and South East Scotland Rep for environmental charity Surfers Against Sewage, and, like many people, he surfs right through the winter at Pease. 'The really difficult thing for us is that it's so hard to pin down how you've got ill,' he says. 'For example, I know somebody who got E coli – she spent a week in hospital and she's pretty sure she got it at Pease Bay. The doctor's view was, "You probably got this from surfing at Pease Bay, but I can't prove it." We don't have any definite statistics, but you won't meet any surfers who surf here regularly who haven't had some sort of bug. I've had sickness, diarrhoea, ear infections, eye infections . . . and I'm one of the lucky ones.'

Steele takes me out to the treatment plant at Cove. The plant itself is situated on a narrow headland, and the pipe issuing out of it enters the water at the foot of the steep, crumbling cliffs beneath before heading out to sea. 'At places like this in England, the UV is left on year-round,' says Steele. 'The Environment Agency have said to English water companies, you need to leave it on all year unless you can prove there are no recreational water users'. But then you come north of the Border and the Scottish Environmental Protection Agency [SEPA] don't make the same demands.'

When I contacted Scottish Water, a spokesman said: 'Cove waste water treatment works is fully compliant with all necessary legislation.' So I got onto SEPA and asked if there was any chance they might follow the Environment Agency's lead in future, making year-round UV treatment mandatory at sewage treatment plants close to year-round recreational bathing areas. SEPA's Environmental Quality Manager replied: 'As there isn't a statutory driver, mandatory year-round UV treatment at sewage treatment plants close to year-round recreational bathing areas is unlikely.' Which sounds a lot like: 'There's no law that says we have to make them do it.' The SEPA spokesman added that he didn't believe Cove sewage treatment works pose 'a significant risk' to water users as they are located 'at a distance from the Pease Bay area'. SEPA also provided evidence of three water quality tests carried out in the winter of 2011, one in February, one in March and one in April, that seem to bear this out.

So what's going on? Either a) surfers at Pease are getting ill because they're ingesting pathogens coming from the sewage treatment plant at Cove, in which case the Scottish Government should perhaps take a careful look at its 'statutory drivers'. Or b) SEPA is right, and sewage that has only received secondary treatment doesn't 'pose a significant risk' to health, in which case, surely, using UV treatment at Cove during the summer months represents a huge waste of taxpayers' money – and should be stopped right away.

*

If the water at Pease is indeed safe to swim in when the UV treatment is turned off in the winter, why would Scottish Water bother spending money to have it turned on in the summer? To get an answer to that question, I began by calling the Senior Press Officer at Scottish Water. 'Right now this minute,' I said, 'is the water at Pease Bay safe to swim in? Would you come down there with me now and go splash about in the shorebreak?' 'It's freezing!' he replied. 'Yeah, but with a wetsuit you can go in all year round. Would you go into the water at Pease now?' 'Yes, definitely. I'd have no qualms about it.' 'So why do Scottish Water switch the UV treatment on in the bathing season? If it's safe now, what's the point of having UV treatment for the bathing season?' 'So that you know, it ensures that, erm . . . see, you . . . you're coming from a position where you're saying . . . well, you're not saying it but you're assuming . . .'

I was subsequently instructed to put any further questions I might have in an email, so I turned to the Environment Quality Manager at SEPA. I asked him if he thought the water at Pease was safe outside the bathing season. 'It's as safe as anybody can say,' he replied. 'Never say never, of course, but in the general sense of normal environmental quality the bathing water is as safe as it could be. The sewage [at Cove] is treated all year round by normal technology, but it gets this additional sort of polishing just for the bathing season – which it actually doesn't need, but it gets it as part of a belt-and-braces approach.'

So if the water at Pease is safe without the UV, by using UV in the summer are we just blowing a load of tax bucks on something we don't actually need? 'Possibly, yeah. I think all the evidence we've had so far is that there isn't any obvious benefit [to UV treatment]. But that's just my personal opinion based on an understanding of all the inputs.' So there you have it. According to SEPA's head of Environment Quality, UV screening at Cove during the summer isn't strictly necessary. The only reason it happens at all is because an EU Directive demands it: 'The European Bathing Directive is specifically targeted at bathing, and as such that's really where our focus is,' the SEPA spokesman told me.

He also pointed to three winter water quality tests carried out by Sepa in 2011 (one in February, one in March and one in April) that show water quality at Pease to be within the recommended limits, and he suggested that surfers are more likely to be made sick by contaminated runoff from the land around Pease ending up in the two burns that flow into the bay than by effluent from the sewage treatment plant at Cove.

*

So how do Surfers Against Sewage respond to SEPA's stats? SEPA's position that UV treatment during the bathing season may in fact be a waste of money is based, in part, on water quality tests carried out in the winter and spring of 2011. On 15 February a water sample was taken from the bay at Pease and tested for pathogens. The test was repeated on 16 March and 13 April. On each occasion, pathogen levels recorded were well within the guideline (excellent) standard as set out in the EU's Bathing Water Directive.

But according to Andy Cummins, Campaigns Director at SAS, these findings are of questionable value. 'SEPA is over-simplifying a complex system,' he says. 'I'm concerned that by jumping to these conclusions, they are either misleading the public or showing a lack of understanding of the environment. What SEPA do is pick the spot which they feel is the most heavily-used spot along a given beach, and they'll use that one spot as their sampling point. They'll go out to a metre depth and they'll submerge a 100ml bottle 30cms below the water. All you'll be able to tell from that sample is what the water was like at that one spot along the beach at that one point in time.'

Cummins sent me a hugely detailed study carried out in 2010 at Godrevy Beach in Cornwall by the Environment Agency (the English equivalent of SEPA), Cornwall Council and Southwest Water, with SAS as a partner organisation. Samples were taken at 20 different spots on 23 different days between July and October. 'We saw samples taken on the same day at the same time across 20 different points giving dramatically different results,' he says. 'We saw failures of the EU directive and passes and guideline [excellent] passes – all along the same stretch of beach.'

The sheer volume of data gathered at Godrevy – four different spreadsheets, each containing over 500 units of data – does make the total of six units of data gathered by SEPA appear somewhat insubstantial by comparison. 'The burden of proof needs to be in the favour of water users,' says Cummins. 'Let's have UV treatment turned on year round, and then if Scottish Water want to reduce the level of treatment, let's make sure there's a detailed analysis of Pease Bay first. When we've got that information, we can all sit around a table and say, "Let's have a common sense approach here – these are the true impacts". But we simply can't do that with the information we've got so far.'

The Boardwise fire and the end of an era

FOR many years, the Boardwise surf shop on Lady Lawson Street was an important dot on Scotland's surfing map, not just because it was one of only a few places in the country where you could go to buy functional gear, but also because Brian and Sarah Stark, who ran it, always seemed to be up to date with what everyone was up to. It was an important part of my personal psychogeography of Edinburgh, too. For many years I used to walk past it on my way to work, and it was often a place I'd go to get last-minute birthday presents for the surfing people in my life, to the point where my panicky right-before-closing-time visits became a bit of a running joke. The fire that destroyed the place in the summer of 2016 didn't just force Edinburgh's sideways-sliding community to start shopping online, it also destroyed a museum's worth of surfing and snowboarding memorabilia and removed an important part of the scene's social jigsaw puzzle. Sure, some anonymous online retailer might be able to offer you free delivery, but will they be able to tell you who just scored perfect waves on a recent Hebridean adventure? No, sadly, they will not.

31 March 2017

On the evening of 25 August last year, Brian and Sarah Stark, who run the Boardwise surf and snowboard shop on Edinburgh's Lady Lawson Street, got a call from their neighbours at the

Timberyard restaurant to tell them their building was on fire. 'We got there in 20 minutes,' remembers Sarah, 'but by then there were already nine [fire brigade] units outside.' The blaze was eventually extinguished at 4am on the morning of the 26th, but by that time the damage had been done. Thousands of pounds worth of stock had been destroyed – either burned by the flames, melted by the intense heat or ruined by the smoke. More devastating still, it seemed that over three decades of board-riding history might also have been lost.

Set up by Brian and his dad in 1983 (at that time selling predominantly windsurfing gear), and now owned by Brian and his sister, Carolyn Corrigan, Boardwise was never really just a shop. Yes, it has always been in the business of buying and selling stock, but over the years Brian and Sarah had also built up a collection of rare and notable surfboards, snowboards, skateboards and other memorabilia, much of which was also destroyed. That said, it has been possible to salvage a few important items from the wreckage. When I visit Boardwise almost seven months on from the fire, the long, arduous process of stripping out all the fire-damaged fixtures and fittings is almost complete. Brian tells me they've had to get rid of 20 tonnes of debris – he knows the figure, he says, because he's had to pay £200 per tonne to dispose of it. Before the fire, Boardwise used to feel like a treasure trove bursting at the seams with desirable gear – wetsuits on the left as you came in through the door, surfboard rack on the right, then walk straight ahead to the counter and turn left to find enough snowboard kit to see you through 1,000 winters. Now, though, the shop is an empty cavern, stripped right back to its mid-19th century stone walls, and the smell of smoke hangs heavy in the air. In spite of everything, however, there are still a few clues as to the building's past. On the banister at the top of the stairs leading down to the basement, for example, there's an old Sola wetsuits sticker dating from the 1980s, miraculously unscathed.

Sarah takes me down into the basement storeroom where the fire began. 'It started just over there,' she says, pointing to a corner that would have been directly underneath the spot where the snowboard rack used to stand. 'We had a dehumidifier on because we'd had a flood two weeks before. After we'd ascertained the cause of the leak we had to get hold of a dehumidifier to get rid of the smell and the dampness.' Unfortunately the dehumidifier was faulty – faulty enough to take out the entire shop. Still, not everything was lost. In another area of the basement there's a small collection of vintage snowboards – damaged, but still recognisable. 'That board there is quite an old one,' says Sarah, pointing to a slightly singed Burton Brushie Cruzin 153, designed by halfpipe pioneer Jeff Brushie and handmade in Vermont in the mid-1990s. Beside it is a limited edition Lib Tech Travis Rice Art of Flight Pro model, as used by Rice in the iconic *Art of Flight* movie. Before the fire it was in mint condition and still in its wrapper; now it has large scorch marks all along its deck. 'It was worth a lot of money,' says Sarah, 'now it's not.' There's also an Apo board that once bore custom graphics by Brian Froud, along with the artist's signature – one of only three he signed. Now, though, most of the board's topsheet is burned beyond repair, and the fantastical illustrations can only really be seen towards the tail.

But Brian and Sarah are doing their best to stay positive: they hope to throw a 'big bonfire party' on 25 August this year, then reopen the shop the following day. And then we'll go 'what happened to that year?' jokes Brian. And although a lot of historic artefacts were lost in the fire, there have been one or two intriguing finds in the aftermath. A yellowing newspaper front page discovered during the clean-up operation dates from 1917. 'Rapid progress beyond Peronne' reads the headline, 'British reach points ten miles east of the Somme.' Nobody seems sure what purpose the building was originally intended for, but one theory is that the high ceilings, grand cornices and multiple fireplaces might have originally housed some sort of gentleman's club.

And then there's the dead bunny. In order to ensure the fire had been extinguished, fire crews had to rip out chunks of the ceiling to check under the rafters. After they'd gone, Sarah climbed a ladder to have a look and 'nearly screamed the place down' when she discovered a rabbit skeleton. The National Museum of Scotland is sending an expert to investigate, but apparently builders often used to seal dead creatures into new buildings to ward off evil spirits. For now, though, 'bony bunny' is staying in the shop, just in case.

Surfboard shaper Jason Burnett on form, function and fibreglass art

THIS story could easily have ended up in the culture chapter of this book. Not only are the surfboards Jason Burnett shapes works of art in themselves, he also makes artworks with materials left over from the glassing process. In essence, though, he's someone who makes a living from crafting functional sports equipment for paying customers. That's not to say that he isn't also an artist, but his ultimate goal is to create boards that work for his clients – a focus on function over form. The fact that the boards he makes also happen to look spectacular no doubt satisfies his inner artist, while also keeping his clients coming back for more.

21 March 2018

There ain't no surf in Portobello, as The Valves sang in 1977, but there was a surfboard exhibition just up the road in Leith last week, courtesy of east coast shaper Jason Burnett. In the white cube-ish exhibition space at Custom Lane, just off Commercial Street, Burnett had six of his hand-crafted creations suspended from the ceiling by wires, and he was also showcasing some of the artworks he makes from leftover polyester resin, one of the substances used in the board-making process: sculptures, bowls and even a psychedelic table-top, each one a unique product of the same strange alchemy that gives surfboards their luminous, waterproof finish.

An artfully shot video playing on a loop in the gallery showed the various stages that go into creating a custom board: first a polyurethane blank – a sort of rough, generic outline of a surfboard – is carefully cut and sanded into the desired shape; then fins are added to give the board forward momentum (or fin boxes inserted into the underside of the board so that removable fins can be fitted later); then the finished design is covered in layers of fibreglass and resin, which, when dry and sanded smooth, form a protective, watertight shell. Coloured resins are added at this final stage if required, and it's by experimenting with these unpredictable substances that Burnett gradually found himself making art objects as well as surfboards.

Several of the works on show at Custom Lane were abstract wall panels, made by pouring surplus resin directly onto pieces of canvas. One of them bore more than a passing resemblance to an aerial photograph of a tropical reefbreak, with coral heads visible under aquamarine water. 'It evolved that way,' says Burnett. 'I poured different colours of resin onto the canvas, moved them about and then watched what happened. The resin takes about 20 minutes to gel up, and even after that it's still doing stuff.' The surfboards in the exhibition were in a mixture of styles – some were nods to famous shapers of the past while others represented the cutting edge of contemporary design. At just 4ft 6in long, the Flex Spoon Kneeboard was the most out-there of the six. Inspired by the craft shaped and ridden by California surfer, sailor and inventor George Greenough, star of the 1973 surf film Crystal Voyager, it only has foam in the nose and along the rails; the central portion of the board is just resin and fibreglass, built up slowly, layer upon painstaking layer. 'There's about 16 or 18 layers of fibreglass at the back,' Burnett says, 'and it gets less and less towards the front.'

'This board was way ahead of its time,' he continues. 'Because there's no foam here [in the centre of the board] you're more connected to the surface of the wave.'

Another reference to the history of surfboard design, Burnett's 7ft Mini-Gun was inspired by the needle-like Lightning Bolt boards that Gerry Lopez built in the 1970s to help him rocket through the grinding barrels of Pipeline, the infamous reefbreak on the Hawaiian island of Oahu. And the board's sleek contours aren't the only reference to its heritage – there's a subtle lightning bolt shape just visible on board's marbled, multi-coloured deck, and another even more subtle one sanded into its all-black underside. 'This board would be fast,' says Burnett, 'but hard to turn. One for a good day.'

Among the more modern designs on show were two asymmetrical boards – one at 6ft, the other at 6ft 4in. These had a straighter toe-side edge to give greater down-the-line speed, but a more rounded heel-side edge, to make backside turns easier. 'If you had curved rails both sides, you wouldn't be able to drive off your toes as fast as you could off that straight rail,' says Burnett. 'But you feel you've got more stability and more control than if you're riding something that's straight both sides.'

Burnett, who works out of a studio in the Newbattle Abbey Business Park, says he didn't have any formal training as an artist. He first got into surfing while swimming competitively for Edinburgh clubs. Next, he started doing ding repairs on his own boards – patching cracks and scrapes with fibreglass and resin – and once he'd mastered that, having a go at shaping felt like a natural progression. There have been many notable shaper-surfer relationships over the years – from Maurice Cole and Tom Curren to Al Merrick and Kelly Slater to Darren Hadley and Mick Fanning – so clearly there's an advantage to developing a relationship with an expert shaper rather than simply buying a board straight off the rack (or – more likely these days – buying one via the internet). Burnett explains why the surfer-shaper relationship still matters: 'Every surfer surfs differently, and everybody's surfing to a different ability as well, so it's about getting something more attuned to them. It's like walking into a store and getting a suit tailored to you – you end up with something that's more attuned to you, and something that's going to help you surf better. And that's what it's all about.'

'I was about to knock it on the head' – a near miss for Edinburgh's wave pool

WITH the benefit of hindsight, it's obvious that Andy Hadden's prediction in this interview that his artificial surfing wave would be up and running on the outskirts of Edinburgh by 2020 proved somewhat optimistic. As we now know, however, following challenges including a global pandemic and an unprecedented period of inflation that sent construction costs soaring, he had his perfect wave up and running by the autumn of 2024. Scottish surfing would never be the same again.

10 May 2018

At the end of last month the much-discussed Wavegarden Scotland project received planning consent from the City of Edinburgh Council, delighting surfers from Coldingham to Thurso. The idea of a perfect surfing wave breaking in a former quarry in Ratho sounds so far-fetched, however, that when I catch up with 36-year-old Andy Hadden, co-founder of Tartan Leisure Ltd, the company which is developing the site, I still feel I have to ask him: is this really happening? 'Yeah,' he says, 'it's been happening in my head for the past five-and-a-half years. I'm the most cynical person in this project and I'm aware of how it sounds in the pub on first hearing so we've tried to play our cards close to our chest until we're satisfied it's going to happen – and we are now, so yeah, we're super excited.'

Occupying the former Craigpark Quarry next-door to the Edinburgh International Climbing Arena (EICA), the new, state-of-the-art wave pool will be able to serve up waves in a wide range of shapes and sizes at the rate of 1,000 waves per hour, making it ideal for experts and beginners alike. It's estimated that it will create 130 jobs and generate up to £11 million for the local economy each year, and it will also provide Scotland's competitive surfers with a world class training facility. Mark Boyd, captain of the Scottish Surfing Team, has said it will give elite competitors 'a huge edge when it comes to future competitions' and it's not hard to see why: in the ocean every wave is different, but imagine how much more quickly it would be possible to perfect a tricky new manoeuvre if you could surf exactly the same wave again and again until you got it right. 'We plan to be open in 2020,' says Hadden, 'which coincides nicely with surfing becoming an Olympic sport for the first time.'

But before we leap too far into the future, let's travel back in time to 2012, when Hadden was sitting at a desk in Birmingham, working for the property company Colliers International. 'I was working in insolvency,' he says, 'so helping businesses out of liquidation and administration and then dealing with their assets. It was really at the blunt end of the recession, but while it was very grim it was also a great learning experience in business.'

One day, an internal memo appeared about a surf park in Wales. Seán Young, the head of Colliers destination consulting department in London, was doing the first feasibility study for what eventually became Surf Snowdonia. To most of the people at Colliers who received it, that email would have been little more than a curiosity, but for Hadden – a keen east coast surfer, originally from Edinburgh, who was at that time making regular car-camping missions to Cornwall to satisfy his wave-cravings – it was a life-changing moment.

'I got straight on the phone to Seán in London and said, "Come on now, are you having a laugh?"' he remembers. 'But here was this very credible guy who had done feasibility studies for all sorts of international destinations, and he said, "Andy, this is a business, this is a standalone surf park and it's legitimate."' Initially, Hadden looked into developing a wave pool near Dunbar, but after six months of feasibility work in 2013, concluded the site would be too far from major population centres. As part of his research, however, he had spoken to various outdoor sports centres in the area including the EICA in

Ratho. 'I was about to knock it on the head,' he says, 'but the guys at the climbing arena said to me, "Have you ever checked out the landowners next door? It's the Brewsters." I said "Scott Brewster?" They said, "Yeah," and I said, "I played rugby with him! I've been on a lads' holiday with him!" So I phoned him up and said, "Scott, just give me a minute here, I've got an idea . . ."'

With their planning application approved, the two co-founders of Tartan Leisure Ltd are now within touching distance of achieving their dream, but Hadden is keen for people to understand that this is a passion project, not simply a money-making exercise. As a surfer on Scotland's fickle east coast for many years, he considers he's done 'all the hard yards that everyone else does' and therefore understands what a facility like this will mean to an average Scottish surfer. 'We're not some big bad developer,' he says, 'absolutely not. I'm just a surfer who wanted one of these for Christmas.'

From beach huts to surf centres:
the infrastructure of stoke

UNTIL very recently, Scotland didn't have much in the way of what you might call permanent surfing infrastructure. Sure, there were a few surf shops, but that was about it. Surf schools were dotted around the coast, but these tended to be modest, portable affairs. For many years Dunbar-based Sam Christopherson ran his Coast to Coast school out of the back of a van, and for a time Craig Sutherland had a Suds Surf School horse box full of gear parked on the machair beside Ballevulin on Tiree that worked on a sort of digital honesty box system – if you were on the island and he wasn't you could just give him a call, let him know how many boards and wetsuits you needed and transfer the funds when you were done with them. By 2019 though, vans and beach-side horse boxes were starting to be replaced by actual, physical structures. For youngsters beginning their surfing journeys today, whether in Dunbar or Thurso or Tiree, it probably feels as if these buildings have always been there. For those who were around before any of them existed, though, they still feel like exciting novelties.

2 May 2019

Surfing, famously, is a sport that leaves no trace. In 10,000 years' time, when archaeologists from another galaxy land on our planet and start looking for signs of what went wrong with human civilisation, it's entirely possible that they will discover the crumbling remains of mighty football stadiums in cities all over the world, but they'd be doing well to find much physical evidence of surfing. True, if they were lucky they might just stumble upon the remains of Kelly Slater's artificial wave pool in the middle of California (or, indeed, the one that's currently under construction at Ratho, just outside Edinburgh) and wonder why, on a planet mostly comprised of oceans, anybody felt the need to recreate ocean waves on dry land.

Apart from the wave pools, though, surf architecture tends to be limited to fairly rudimentary structures on or near the beach. In surfing hotspots like Australia and California, there are lifeguard towers, built to give a clear view of the surf zone, and in chillier, less crowded places, like here in Scotland, there are sometimes beach huts. Like the one built a couple of years ago at Balevullin on Tiree, these tend to be simple wooden affairs, designed to provide a bit of shelter from the elements and a place to store gear. Recently, however, Scotland's surf huts have been getting considerably more ambitious – to the extent that it's probably time to stop referring to them as 'huts'.

In Thurso, overlooking the celebrated reef break at Thurso East, an impressive-looking surf shelter is being constructed under the aegis of the North Shore Surf Club, on land donated by Lord Thurso. Boasting toilets, showers, storage space, an office, changing rooms and an elevated judging area for contests, it is now nearing completion and should revolutionise the experience of surfing at Scotland's most famous break. It should also make it easier to hold competitions, such as the Scottish National Surfing Championships, which took place there last month.

Meanwhile, about 300 miles down the road in Dunbar, the Belhaven Surf Centre at the south end of Belhaven Bay is also well on the way to opening its doors. Work on the £250,000 building started last autumn, and, all being well, it should be completed and opened some time in the summer. The centre will boast a multi-purpose education room, an office, storage, heated changing rooms, toilets and warm showers, all at ground floor level, and it will also include two first-floor rooms, one with stunning views across Belhaven Bay. The centre will be run on a not-for-profit basis, providing a home for various surf- and beach-related organisations and businesses based in the area, including Coast to Coast Surf School, East Lothian Countryside Ranger Service, The Wave Project and Dunbar Surf Life Saving Club.

Sam Christopherson of Coast to Coast, one of the prime movers behind the scheme, describes it as a dream come true. 'We've always had this concept that we wanted to do something with the rangers,' he says, 'so we could share a space and have environmental education and outdoor adventure running side by side. That's been a theme since we started the surf school in 2004. Three years ago there was a change in the council – countryside and sport got merged – so there was suddenly somebody interested in sport in charge of countryside too, and that opened some doors for us.' The council drew the attention of Sam and the rangers to a plot of land by the beach at the south end of Belhaven Bay, close to the infamous 'Bridge to Nowhere', that had been lying vacant for many years, and asked if they'd like to lease it. 'We were like, yeah, that would be amazing,' says Christopherson, 'because it gives us a facility right on the beach. They gave us the lease of that space for 35 years and then we went off to see what we could do in the way of funding and how we could build a building that would house all the different needs that there were in the area. The surf school had to create a new social enterprise called Belhaven Surf Centre in order to oversee the whole thing – it's building the building and managing its long-term use, so the building is actually in the community for the long term. There's no profit in terms of the surf school owning the land – and after 35 years it goes back to the council.'

Christopherson is keen to stress that the thing that makes this project unique is the range of organisations that will be using the space at the same time. Far from being a mere surf hut, the Belhaven Surf Centre will combine sports coaching, environmental education and the outreach and inclusion work of surf therapy charity The Wave Project under the same roof. 'To our knowledge this is the first coastal building in the UK with so many different interests in it and the potential for cross-education is huge,' he says. 'Users of the building, whether a new surfer, a high school pupil or a pensioner, can come for an activity but leave having learned about coastal safety or the local environment or having helped change someone's life as a volunteer on an inclusive project.'

Brian Allen of the environmental charity Surfers Against Sewage, who will also be using the building, describes it as a 'game-changer' for the local area, and 'an amazing new space, ideal to host future beach cleans and environmental education.' East Lothian Council Countryside Ranger Tara Sykes, meanwhile, believes the new centre is going to be 'integral to fostering a sense of ownership in Dunbar's coastline and encouraging more activity outdoors in a sustainable and environmentally friendly way.' 'It will give us fantastic facilities for outdoor education, surf safety and sports performance development,' says Christopherson, 'as well as environmental education and pushing the environmental message. It's almost like the dream ticket.'

The rise and rise of
North Coast Watersports

IN ONE respect, Iona McLachlan and Finn MacDonald opened their new Thurso-based surf school North Coast Watersports at the worst possible time: right before the Covid-19 pandemic. However, as McLachlan points out in this interview, conducted just after her Scottish National Surfing Championships win in 2019, in another respect their timing could hardly have been better: by 2019 the North Coast 500 tourist driving route was indeed 'kicking off' and since the easing of lockdown restrictions it has brought a veritable tidal wave of tourists to Sutherland and Caithness. As a result, North Coast Watersports has now grown to include paddleboard adventures and RIB tours as well as surf lessons, and the business has picked up a whole host of awards.

28 May 2019

For a few golden years from 2006 to 2011, the town of Thurso played host to a professional surfing contest sponsored by surf-wear giant O'Neill, known first as the Highland Open and later as the Coldwater Classic. During this period, some of the best surfers in the world visited Caithness to compete in the thumping waves of Thurso East and Brims Ness, from veterans like 2000 world surfing champion Sunny Garcia to new kids on the block like John John Florence – a hotly-tipped youngster when he first visited Thurso who went on to win back to back world titles in 2016 and 2017. In 2012, O'Neill announced it was cancelling the Classic for 'the foreseeable future' in order to direct resources elsewhere, but those contests certainly made their mark, putting Thurso firmly on the world surfing map and also inspiring more locals to give the sport a try.

One young schoolgirl who paid particularly close attention to the last ever O'Neill event in 2011 was Iona McLachlan, now 19. 'I remember the last year of that competition,' she says. 'I hadn't started surfing then, but I remember meeting the surfers and that's when I was just like, "This is really cool, I really want to get involved."' McLachlan didn't just 'get involved', she quickly became an unstoppable force on the junior competitive circuit, winning the Under-18 Girls division three years in a row at the Scottish National Surfing Championships. And last month she went one better, winning the Women's Open title at the Scottish Nationals in a final that featured two previous winners, Shoana Blackadder and Phoebe Strachan. When the people who put on major sports events talk about 'legacy' this, surely, is the kind of thing they mean. 'I didn't expect to get anywhere,' says McLachlan of her most recent win. 'I've only entered the women's once before because I'd always been in the Under-18s Girls category so I just did it for a bit of fun. . . but yeah, I ended up winning it which was great.'

McLachlan's victory was particularly noteworthy as the final was held in solid surf at the Cove at Brims Ness – a fast, shallow wave that breaks over slabs of granite. 'I was pretty nervous,' says McLachlan. 'I'm not really a fan of big, heavy waves, I try to avoid them. The waves that day were quite shifty, too, breaking in different places all the time, and that makes it much harder to judge which waves are going to be OK to surf.'

In spite of the tricky conditions, footage of McLachlan recorded on the day shows her looking focused but relaxed, carving fast, tight turns in order to keep herself in the power pocket of the wave. 'It was low tide when we were surfing,' she says. 'We couldn't really hear the commentator so we were pretty much blind with what the scores were. I managed to catch a couple of waves at the start and I knew they were reasonably decent, but then I got a bit confused with time – I thought we had ages left and then I suddenly realised we only had about two minutes left. Anyway, in the last couple of minutes I managed to get a second back-up wave which I think was just enough to get me into first place, so it was very close!'

McLachlan has spent the last year travelling the world with her partner Finn MacDonald (who regular readers will know as one half of Tiree's surfing super-duo alongside Ben Larg) and while they were on the road they ticked off bucket list spots including Hikkaduwa in Sri Lanka and Raglan Bay in New Zealand. They also spent time working as instructors at the Aotearoa Surf School on New Zealand's North Island and, inspired by what they saw there, are now setting up their own surf school, North Coast Watersports, based in Thurso. 'We're doing most of our lessons at Dunnet Beach,' says McLachlan, 'because the waves there are nice and easy for learning on, and we'll mostly be teaching beginners but some improvers too. I think up here we really need some outdoor activities for tourists, because it's all really kicking off with the North Coast 500 [driving route]. It will be good to have something for locals as well. Even people who have lived here their whole lives can sometimes have no idea there's any surf scene, or that there are waves up here that are good to surf.'

Wax on, wax off – the organic adventures of the Braw boys

WHEN I spoke to Oscar James in June 2021, he was sounding pretty upbeat, and rightly so. He and his business partners at Edinburgh-based Braw Surf, Donald Inglis and Tonie Nguyen, had set themselves the not-inconsiderable challenge of developing a surf wax that was both organic and would work in cold conditions, and after a long and tricky testing period, much complicated by Covid-19 restrictions, they seemed to have nailed it. Their Celtic Wax subsequently went on sale in surf shops all around Scotland and England and online, creating guilt-free stoke for countless happy customers. Sadly, however, by the autumn of that year the pressure of manufacturing the product at scale had started to take its toll.

In a post on the Braw Surf Facebook page, the trio wrote: 'A plateau has been reached. After multiple lockdowns, jobs & futures in question, what has been a relentless assault on the mind and spirit is slowly coming to an end, and like many others, we are reeling in the wake of it. We no longer have the time or knowledge to develop this wax further on our own. Up to this point every single block that has been made and distributed has come, handmade, from a small kitchen in a Leith flat. The effort was substantial, considering the volume of sales keeps increasing, and it started to take over. The fallout: we have pulled the wax (and entire online shop) from our website. . . This is not a decision we have taken lightly, but there comes a time when you have to put your own heid first, and that's what we've done.'

There was a suggestion in their post that Braw might return, but at time of writing their website remains down. Still, in identifying a gap in the market and developing a successful product to fill it, the Braw team achieved something much bigger and better-resourced organisations have frequently tried and failed to do. It's also notable that the Braw project originated at Edinburgh Napier University – we'll be hearing more about its role as a hotbed of surf industry innovation later in this chapter. . .

12 June 2021

Thanks to the second verse of the Beach Boys' 1963 classic 'Surfin' USA', the concept of waxing a surfboard is now familiar to millions of non-surfers all around the globe. The question of what exactly this process entails, however, doesn't seem to be quite so universally understood. Perhaps because skiers wax the bottoms of their skis in order to make them go faster, a lot of people mistakenly assume it's the same deal with surfing. (No shame if that was you by the way: the long-time Hawaii resident Paul Theroux just published his first surfing novel, *Under the Wave at Waimea*, and even he and his editors seem to be under the impression that the purpose of surf wax is to make boards go faster.)

So, just to make sure we're all on the same page: surfers rub wax onto the top of their boards (known as the deck) to give them grip in the water. Without wax, the surface of a surfboard would be about as slippery as an ice rink, and the sport of surfing would be the eighth slapstick wonder of the world. You can spend hundreds of pounds on a surfboard, but without a little bar of wax costing a couple of quid, you'll get nowhere. For decades, the surf wax market has been dominated by a few big brands, most of which delight in riffing on the onanistic undertones of wax application on their packaging. Made in California since 1972, Mr Zogg's Sex Wax claims to be 'the best for your stick' while Mrs Palmers, made in Australia, encourages users to 'Give it a rub – the feeling just keeps getting better.' These traditional waxes tend to be made from either paraffin wax or soy wax, neither of which are renewable resources and both of which involve the use of petrochemicals in their manufacture. However, there are renewable alternatives, and a new Scottish company called Braw is looking to capitalise on this gap in the market while also sidestepping the dubious Carry On vibes.

Braw was founded in January 2020 by three surfers who met at Napier University and realised they had complementary skills: Donald Inglis, Tonie Nguyen and Oscar James. Inglis studied business and marketing at Napier; Nguyen is a designer, originally from Germany, who moved to Scotland to study and stayed on afterwards to work on Braw; and James's background is in sports media, mainly photography and video work – we have him to thank for the slick video footage of this year's British Surfing Championships, held at Thurso East. 'We all met through the surf club at university,' says James. 'We went on a holiday together to Spain – I think that was in the summer of 2019 – and we all got into surfing at around the same time.'

'The business idea only came about last year,' he continues. 'Duncan had lived in South Africa, and while he was there somebody taught him a recipe for organic surf wax. Surfing in Scotland is still a niche thing, and a lot of the surf waxes you buy don't really work here, even the cold water ones – when they get really cold they just get super hard and then you can't get them onto your board. It's just one of these things that everybody accepts about surfing in Scotland, but we thought we'd try and do better.'

So, Braw's goal is to make a wax that works in cold water and is also sustainable. In order to achieve this, a lot of pains-taking research and development was required, and ultimately this meant finding some willing product testers, waxing up their boards with the latest prototypes and then sending them out into the North Sea. A video on the Braw website shows how much work goes into a test day, not just for the surfers trialling the different waxes – in this case Simon Olsson and Hugo Spinola – but also for the crew back on the beach, who have to de-wax and then re-wax boards in between surfs and also keep meticulous notes on what worked and what didn't. 'That day we had nine or ten variations,' says James. 'It's pretty hard on the boys – they surf for a bit, come out of the water, grab their other boards that we've already waxed up and then go straight back in. That day they were surfing for about four hours.'

After trialling 'between 50 and 60 variations' the Braw crew have just launched a product they believe is a winner: their all-new Celtic wax. Without giving away the secret recipe, James is able to tell me that it includes bees' wax, either coconut oil or rape seed oil, depending on availability, and pine resin. 'It's all done by hand,' he says. 'All we need is a gas hob and we can make it pretty much anywhere. It's not like we're going to become a mass operation – we just wanted to see if it was possible to make it and if people would want to buy it, and so far it's going pretty well.'

How Staunch Industries channelled the spirit of the kelpie

SOME weeks, my 900-word outdoors column slot in the *Scotsman Magazine* feels about the right length. Occasionally, when I'm pushed for time and winging things a bit, it feels too long. Mostly, though, it feels too short – and this was very much the case when I was writing up this interview with designer, entrepreneur, surfer, spear-fisherman and all-round force of nature Will Beeslaar. In March 2023, when I visited the new shop and design studio he and his partner Janeanne Gilchrist had just opened in Leith, we chatted for so long I could easily have filled three times as much space. Will's enthusiasm for the sea is infectious, and his love for the North Sea in particular is intense. Even though he gets to surf the legendary waves at Jeffrey's Bay whenever he returns home to South Africa, he's just as passionate about scoring perfect waves in south-east Scotland (a rarer event), and because he can spear-fish through the mostly waveless Scottish summers, he always has a reason to be in or around the sea. In Hawaii, someone who is connected to the ocean through multiple disciplines is known as a waterman – it's about the highest compliment you can bestow, and it could certainly be said to apply to Will, always North Sea powered, whether above or below the water.

18 March 2023

Whether you realise it or not, if you've lived in Scotland for the last decade or so, chances are you will have come into contact with the design work of Staunch Industries. If you've ridden on the Borders Railway since it reopened in 2015 (or even just seen its new-look carriages shuttling between Edinburgh and Tweedbank) you'll be familiar with the colourful Staunch-designed livery, incorporating a range of Borders iconography. If you've visited the giraffes at Edinburgh Zoo since they arrived in 2021, you'll probably have noticed Staunch's stylised take on the African savanna inside their enclosure. And if you've had to take your kids to the paediatric A&E unit of St John's Hospital in Livingston recently, and felt your heart lift a little at the calming tree and bird motifs on the walls, you have Staunch to thank.

Their work appears on smaller-scale canvases too. If you're a fan of Glen Lyon Coffee, ethically sourced and roasted in small batches in Aberfeldy, Staunch designed the imposing stag on the packaging – not to mention the metal camping mugs available on the company's website. And did you ever wonder who was behind the cans for Pilot's Leith Lager, with a multitude of Leith landmarks worked into the design? Yup, that'd be Staunch again.

Before they became the go-to guys for everything from major infrastructure projects to Hot Wheels toy cars, however (yes, they've designed for Hot Wheels too) Staunch were a Scotland-specific surf brand, selling apparel to cold-water wave-riders for whom the slogan 'North Sea Powered' speaks of a lot more than just oil and gas. They've also been the official gear sponsor of the Scottish Surfing Federation, supplying stylish kit for the national surf team. And later this month they'll be returning to their roots, with the opening of a new showroom in Leith, a retrospective exhibition and the launch of a new outdoor clothing range inspired by their love of the life aquatic.

Staunch are artist and designer Will Beeslaar, who originally hails from South Africa, and Leith-born photographer and producer Janeanne Gilchrist, and the official opening of their Bernard Street HQ has been a long time coming, postponed first by the tram works and then by the pandemic. 'It's difficult sometimes to work out where you're going as a creative,' says Beeslaar. 'My thing when we set up Staunch was to have a little Scottish surf brand that's independently owned. It's obviously easy to say you're going to do something, though, but to actually do it can be very difficult. And to make products as well. . . as a designer, if you're just working in a commercial environment and you have clients coming in saying "design me a logo" or whatever, it's easy to talk the talk, but to be actually physically involved in making the products as well, taking them to market, marketing them . . . it can sometimes be extremely challenging. Most people would just quit, right? But this has not been our path. There's been a lot of things we've learned along the way, and we're hoping with this exhibition that we can kinda roll it all into one and show that off – show our journey off.'

Surfing, freediving and spearfishing aren't just hobbies for Beeslaar and Gilchrist – they are a big part of their identities and also, as Beeslaar puts it, 'an integral part of the creative process'. You can see this in Gilchrist's atmospheric underwater photography, which won her the prestigious JD Fergusson Art Award award in 2016; and you can see it in Beeslaar's designs for the new Staunch clothing range, from an octopus who gets tangled up with a mirror image of himself, creating some freestyle Celtic knotwork in the process, to a giant anglerfish and a tiny diver swimming beside the slogan: 'The deeper you go, the bigger they grow.'

Right at the centre of the Staunch design universe, meanwhile, is the kelpie – a sort of unofficial logo which Beeslaar has returned to again and again over the years. 'One of our first designs was the kelpie,' he says. 'It really struck a chord with people and ever since then I've been working on this brand as you would do for a commercial client, always tweaking it, always changing it, always refining it, putting it under pressure and building this diamond out of it. There's not been a week when I haven't been working on it, but through it all I couldn't work out, "Why do we keep being drawn back to this kelpie thing?" Then I was up north riding big waves and I realised: it's not just the kelpie as in this mythological creature calling you towards the waves to drown you, but it's a sea stallion – it's that spirit of wildness – you can't tame it. It's the spirit of creativity, so that's the thing I'm trying to distil, this spirit of creativity, and I think that resonates with a lot of people.'

Inside the Surf Lab with Dr Brendon Ferrier

I HAD only planned to spend an hour or so with Brendan Ferrier, director of the Surf Lab at Edinburgh Napier University; in the end I was there for the best part of a morning, and could happily have spent a couple of days. Technically I was there to talk about wetsuits, and in particular the project that had seen Ferrier testing several different brands on behalf of the about-to-open Lost Shore inland surfing lake near Ratho. In reality, though, we ended up talking about everything from the minutiae of aerial surfing manoeuvres (Ferrier did a whole PhD on that) to sports psychology. And, of course, we talked about the idea of the partnership between the Surf Lab and Lost Shore, and all the things that could mean for the future. What happens when you plug a state-of-the-art surf park into an intellectual power source the size of a university? It's going to be fascinating to find out.

8 June 2024

This September, Scotland's surfing landscape will be utterly transformed when the £60 million Lost Shore surf resort opens at Ratho just outside Edinburgh – an artificial wave pool serving up as many as 1,000 perfect waves every hour. The concept of a flat spell – a period of calm when there are no waves to surf – will effectively disappear overnight. As of September, Scotland will become a flat-spell free zone. The surf will be up all day, every day, for as long as the folks at Lost Shore keep their state-of-the-art Wavegarden Cove machine running. Clearly, this is a dream-come-true development for Scotland's existing surfing community, but such a modestly-sized group alone (no matter how enthusiastic) would never be enough to sustain a facility on this scale. No, in order for the numbers to stack up, new converts will need to be found, new initiates inducted into the tribe, and in order for these newcomers to get hooked on the sport of kings, they will need to remain as warm as possible for as long as possible while splashing around and finding their surf legs in the new (unheated) facility.

Which is where Dr Brendon Ferrier, head of the newly formed Surf Lab at Edinburgh's Napier University, comes in. A million miles away from the stereotype of the tweedy academic, when he meets me in the reception area at Napier's Sighthill Campus he's wearing jeans, flip-flops and a freshly-minted Surf Lab polo shirt. He and Lost Shore founder Andy Hadden first cooked up the idea for Surf Lab seven years ago, and now their concept of a multi-disciplinary surf research centre, able to draw in expertise from departments right across the university, is starting to bear fruit. Exhibit A: a recently completed piece of work analysing the heat-retaining properties of different wetsuits.

'Andy and the Lost Shore team want to put people who have never tried surfing before in the warmest environment they can,' Ferrier explains, 'so then they'll enjoy it and then they'll come back.' And in order for an outdoor wave pool to thrive all year round in Scotland, the quality of the wetsuits available to hire will be critical. 'They could have gone down the route of "Oh, we'll get that wetsuit because it's the cheapest,"' says Ferrier, 'but then you're not going to get your return business.' To ensure their hire suits are as warm as possible, Lost Shore commissioned Ferrier and the Surf Lab team to test the most suitable products from five leading surf brands. Lost Shore's own operations assistant Alejandro Padro was offered as a guinea pig, and he stoically sat in a bath of iced water measuring just one degree celsius for half an hour wearing each of the suits, while thermometers attached to various parts of his body measured changes in skin temperature.

The winner? Gul's 5/4mm Yulex wetsuit, which gave particularly high temperature readings around the lower back area, thanks in part to its high-performance zip. As an added bonus, in contrast to synthetic rubbers commonly used in wetsuits, such as neoprene (made from petrochemicals) and geoprene (made from mined limestone), Yulex is harvested from natural rubber plantations, reducing carbon emissions by around 80 per cent, so these suits are both warm and green. Lost Shore have now ordered some 700 of them, giving them the largest plant-based rental wetsuit offering anywhere in the world.

The wetsuit test is an impressive example of the way in which the Surf Lab can act as a conduit between academia and the surfing world, and the way Ferrier sees it it's just the beginning of the story. 'My philosophy is that, as a university, we should be here to support the community and help people,' he says. 'So small businesses that don't have the money to do their own R&D, we should be enabled to do that or support them in that – that's the whole idea of Surf Lab.'

Ferrier, 52, is an Australian by birth and a kneeboarder by choice. He gained a PhD in Biomechanics from Edith Cowan University in his home city of Perth, Western Australia, where he also studied as an undergraduate. His thesis was titled *Characteristics and Determinants of Aerial Surfing with Implications for Representative Task Design* and in order to complete it, he tells me, he had to watch and analyse every heat of every contest on surfing's World Championship Tour for a period of three years. As such, he has a deep understanding of the biomechanics behind surfing, and this is something he's now putting to use.

Beside the pool area where he carried out the wetsuit testing, he shows me a machine with a surfboard attached designed to analyse muscle activation during paddling; another nearby machine, he believes – a commonly-found piece of gym equipment – might just prove the ideal bit of kit for strengthening these critical muscles. Other Surf Lab projects currently in the pipeline cover everything from performance psychology to the efficacy of surf therapy. 'The idea is to support anyone who wants to do research around surfing,' he says, 'and [I can] approach colleagues throughout the university, so it can be to do with tourism, engineering, psychology . . . I just try to match people up.'

'It's been a long journey' – reflections
on the road to Lost Shore

IN THE autumn of 2024, when the Lost Shore surf resort opened, Scotland got its first artificial surfing wave and a whole new chapter in the history of Scottish surfing began. With a price tag of £60 million, Lost Shore was the most expensive sports infrastructure project to be completed in the country for more than a decade. It's also a hugely complex and multi-faceted development consisting of many discrete but complementary elements. The thought of trying to cover everything in a single magazine column – the mechanics of the pool, the myriad dining and accommodation options, the way cutting-edge health science research permeates almost every aspect of the operation, and the implications of perfect waves on tap for elite (and not so elite) athletes – brought me out in a cold sweat. Fortunately, *Scotsman Magazine* editor Alison Gray took pity on me and let me lay everything out in a four-part series, each part looking at a specific aspect of the development and based on an interview with a different member of the Lost Shore team.

17, 24, 31 August and 7 September 2024

As director of logistics at the soon-to-be-open Lost Shore surf resort at Ratho, Chris Bain is the man in charge of delivering Scotland's first ever machine-made surfing waves. If all goes to plan, in the very near future it should be possible for surfers from all over Scotland and beyond to enjoy perfect surf whenever they like, without having to wait patiently for Mother Nature to deliver just the right combination of wind, tide and swell.

That arguably makes Bain the most important person in Scottish surfing right now: after all, a lot of very excited surfers have been waiting over a decade for this project to come to fruition.

The so-called Cove technology the Lost Shore team are using in their surf lake was developed by a company called Wavegarden, based near San Sebastián in northern Spain. At Lost Shore, it will create around 1,000 waves per hour, breaking both left and right, each one offering rides of 15–20 seconds. Bain explains how, when he travelled Spain on a fact-finding mission, he was sworn to secrecy about the way the process works in no uncertain terms. However, while he can't go into much detail about the specific ingredients in Wavegarden's secret sauce, he is able to give a general sense of how the new set-up will function. 'You have an engine system that creates a wave through paddles that move through the water,' he says, 'that then reacts off the floor of the pool and onto the sidewalls, pushing a wave along the sidewalls.'

As a general rule, waves break when they hit shallow water and back off when they hit deeper water. The concept for the pool at Ratho is for the waves to break hard and fast for the benefit of more experienced surfers when they first come roaring out of the Cove machine, then to dissipate before reforming nearer to shore, providing gentler, more forgiving waves for beginners. One of the keys to the whole Wavegarden construction process, then, is getting the bathymetry – the shape of the lake bed – just right, and Bain and his team have gone the extra mile to ensure that this part of the equation is sound. 'I think what a lot of people have done is build these quite quickly,' he says, referring to earlier surf lakes which have suffered from troublesome leaks, 'but we've had the benefit of time. It's a long journey that we've been on [the project was first announced a decade ago], but it's given us time to think about how to do this properly, and in a way that a) is never going to lose water and b) isn't going to degrade in any way.'

This kind of attention to detail is mirrored in the approach taken by the Wavegarden team, who are spending a full eight weeks at Ratho fine-tuning their equipment before Lost Shore finally opens to the public. 'They're coming up from Spain to do four weeks of dry commissioning and then four weeks of wet commissioning,' says Bain. 'The dry commissioning is just running the software through the system, running the paddles without any water and making sure that's all fine. When they're happy, the lagoon gets filled and that's when they start wet commissioning.' Also, get this: there's a guy called Julen [he prefers not to give his second name] who earns his living by going round different Wavegardens all over the world as their test pilot. 'When you speak to him, though, he says it's quite frustrating because he has to surf in exactly the same way every time to test the wave. It's quite structured – he can't just have fun.'

You'd think maintenance for something as complex as a wave machine would be a nightmare, but whereas earlier wave pools relied on one large moving element to create waves, the Wavegarden generator has a total of 52 paddles or modules, each working independently. If one breaks down, Bain explains, 'you pull it out, replace it with a spare and nobody knows. Also, they've stress tested one of these modules by running it full-tilt for three months in Spain, and it never broke – and obviously we'd never be running it like that.' The Cove machine can already serve up a wide variety of wave types, but there's no danger of it becoming outdated any time soon. The folks at Wavegarden HQ are constantly refining the wave profiles they can offer, and as this technology evolves the pool at Ratho can evolve along with it. 'There are about 20 different types of waves we can create just now,' says Bain. 'But if a different type of wave is developed, they can just press a button in Spain and that will be sent to all the Wavegardens around the world, so we can trial that wave in our pool.'

*

To understand the pivotal role that health will play at Lost Shore, it's necessary to travel back in time to the spring of 2014, when a young surfer called Jamie Marshall had just become the Scottish co-ordinator for the Wave Project – a charity aiming to improve the mental health of young people through surf therapy. Following successful trials in Cornwall and Devon, the Wave Project was about to make its Scottish debut, and Marshall, working in conjunction with Coast to Coast surf school in Dunbar, had been charged with making it all run smoothly.

'That's how I met Andy Hadden,' says Marshall, Hadden being the founder of Lost Shore. 'I think he was on my second ever round of courses as a volunteer, and he was a bit nervous. He'd done all the training but this was going to be the first time he'd ever tried working with young people. I just said to him, "Look, you love your surfing – just help this young person find that as well." We had this young girl with us who had been involved with the Wave Project for a while but hadn't ever stood up on a board, but she stood up after about five minutes with Andy.'

Over the following decade, Marshall's career in health science and the Lost Shore development have grown in tandem. In September 2022, Marshall completed the world's first ever PhD in Surf Therapy at Edinburgh Napier University – funded by Lost Shore. And now, in addition to his role as a Research Fellow at Napier, Marshall has also taken on a part-time job as Lost Shore's social and health innovation lead, with input into a range of related activities at the resort.

Marshall quotes the official definition of surf therapy: 'the use of surfing as a vehicle for delivering intentional, inclusive, population-specific, and evidenced-based therapeutic structures to promote psychological, physical, and psychosocial wellbeing.' It's a bit of a mouthful, but the bit he really wants to highlight is the word 'intentional'. 'Surfing isn't a silver bullet that fixes everything,' he says, 'but it can be an incredible vehicle for helping people, and I think that's something Andy [Hadden] got very early on. He understood that just building a wave pool isn't enough – we need to make sure we're intentional with the structures around it. So, firstly, we're going to have lots of surf therapy at Lost Shore. We're going to have the Wave Project there from Day One, and we're also partnering with Inclusive Surfing Scotland, who offer adaptive surfing for people with disabilities. For a family to book a disability surf session with us – we want that to feel as easy and as normal as anybody else booking a surf session. In addition to all that, though, our aim is that everyone who visits us leaves feeling a little better than they did when they came. Obviously that makes commercial sense, but this is also where that point about surfing as a vehicle becomes really important. Surfing in the wild has been shown at times to be incredibly exclusive and elitist, so at Lost Shore it's up to us to address all the things around that to make sure it's a really positive experience.'

To that end, Marshall explains that in addition to overseeing the surf therapy side of the business he has also been tasked with 'jumping around all the different departments to make sure that that visitor experience is grounded in the latest scientific research'. Every member of staff, from baristas to lifeguards, will receive positive psychology training.

He has even had input into the health and wellbeing implications of the design of the site.

'In the wave pool world,' he says, 'there's a lot of talk about blue health – that is, people generally feeling better around water – but often it's people talking about things that are incidental to their operations. We want to be intentional about it, so everything about the physical design of the pool has been informed by psychology considerations. For example, where do we want people to be able to lose themselves in the experience without people leering over them with their cellphones?'

The overall goal, then, is to create a place that has a positive impact on everyone who visits. 'Where we've got the intervention stuff, the surf therapy, that's about helping people who are struggling,' he says, 'but that's not enough. That's where psychology's focused for the last 100 years, and we've made huge progress in that, but we also need to spend some time thinking about how we get people from feeling average to happier, and eventually how we get that whole average up.'

*

Towards the end of last year, Lost Shore announced that it had appointed Andy Roger as its CEO. Most recently, Roger had been resort director at the five-star Cameron House on Loch Lomond, and before that he had worked at One Devonshire Gardens in Glasgow, various Malmaison hotels and Hotel du Vin Tunbridge Wells. Fair to say, then, that a professional with more experience of the hospitality sector in Scotland would have been tricky to find.

In terms of food and drink, Roger's concept for Lost Shore is to offer a constantly changing selection of dining options, curated by Edinburgh agency Rogue Village. 'Rogue Village will source the independent kitchens that will come in and work with us,' he explains. 'Two of the kitchens will change every three months and one of the kitchens will change every 12 months. That means that, if you come to visit Lost Shore in the fourth quarter of this year, you'll have three different food offerings to choose from, but if you come back in January only one of those will still be there.'

Broadly-speaking, Roger predicts that there will be three main groups of people looking for food at the resort when it opens: 'People who are surfing and who need something to eat afterwards; people who have come for the overall resort experience; and people who have said "Oh, that restaurant's there, we must go out and try it."' The first three food offerings have been chosen accordingly, with everything from quick, filling food for hungry surfers to more high-end offerings to keep more adventurous foodies happy.

Of the first two kitchens coming in on three-month rotations, one is Five March from the West End of Glasgow, which Roger describes as 'a small-plate concept with a real focus on Scottish ingredients'. The second – also from Glasgow – is Rafa's, specialising in tacos and burritos. 'We've also signed a 12-month agreement with [pizza chain] Civerinos,' says Roger. 'They are predominantly in Edinburgh, so they will be well known to a lot of the Edinburgh market. The fourth pod within the food and beverage space is the bar,' he continues, 'and we'll run that ourselves. We've appointed our own food and beverage manager, who has joined us from Panda & Sons [on Edinburgh's Queen Street], which made the World's 50 Best Bars list last year. We're also working with Pilot brewery, and they are currently brewing a Lost Shore lager.'

When the resort is complete there will be a total of 73 accommodation units on site, with a combined capacity of around 250, and again Roger has divided their expected customers into three main groups: 'People who have come to surf and need somewhere to stay; people who are wanting to come and surf and eat and do a bit of everything; and then people who are perhaps flying off from the airport or going into Edinburgh the next day, but want to stay somewhere out of town.'

In keeping with this, there is a range of self-catering options. On the hilltop above the wave pool there will be 31 three and four-bedroom lodges, each with a kitchen, lounge area and dining area. Then, down by the waterside, there will be three more types of accommodation, all designed by a company called Armadilla, based just south of Edinburgh. The smallest will be the Pods, intended for one or two people. Then there will be two different kinds of accommodation designed to sleep four – Curves and Waves.

The artist's impressions certainly look impressive, but a key test will be how the accommodation links up with the rest of the resort. After all, while you want to offer guests a good view of the waves, you also want people to be able to go surfing without feeling as if they're being watched by hundreds of pairs of eyes. How does Lost Shore square that circle?

'If you're sitting in one of the lodges [on the hilltop],' says Roger, 'if you're in the front row, you'll just about be able to see the bottom of the Cove, but you're certainly not seeing the whites of the eyes of the surfers. Then, with the waterfront accommodation, the closest unit is maybe a bit closer than 100 yards, but most of the surfing happens further back into the Cove. There's a balance of having proximity but not feeling like you're in a

fish bowl, and I think that balance has been really well master-
planned on the site.'

*

It is now almost exactly a decade since Lost Shore founder Andy
Hadden first revealed his plan to create an artificial surfing wave
in Edinburgh. 'It's been a long journey,' he smiles, 'but a great
journey, and we're almost there.' In many ways, the length of
that journey has been a help rather than a hindrance. 'Time has
been one of the best commodities we've had,' Hadden says. 'If
somebody had just handed me a bag of money a few years ago I
would've been tempted just to push the button, but the reality
is that [because of the time it's taken] we've been able to do this
in correctly.'

Having previously worked in investment surveying and insolvency surveying, Hadden has an understanding of both how to
manage financial risks and the consequences of not doing so. As
a result, he says, he has been 'trying to piece this thing together
in the most risk averse way you can possibly do a surf park in
Scotland.' His primary motivation, however, comes not from his
background in finance but his background in sport. 'I come from
a sporting family,' he says. 'When I was growing up, my father
[Frank Hadden, who coached the Scotland Rugby team from
2005–2009] was a PE teacher at an all-boys school, Merchiston.
I grew up in the school grounds there, so I had access to tennis
courts, I could go and do the high jump if I wanted to . . . I took
all this stuff for granted, and it was only later in life that I realised
what it had brought me, and I thought, "Well, not a lot of people
have had these opportunities."'

Dinner table conversations with his father, Hadden says,
would often revolve around elite sports performance, particularly

in 'countries that are punching above their weight'. He also cites two books in particular that have inspired him: *The Goldmine Effect* by Rasmus Ankersen ('about pockets of sporting excellence around the world, so Jamaican sprinters, South Korean female golfers') and *Bounce* by Matthew Syed ('all about the 10,000-hour practice rule'). Creating high-achieving athletes, Hadden believes, has a lot to do with facilities. 'Look at the Fridge Kids down in Sheffield,' he says. 'Jenny Jones and so on. They built a great facility, and then all of a sudden GB started medalling in snowsports. It became really apparent to me that if you could create a world-class surfing facility [in Scotland] there would be nothing stopping us. Do we now have the tools to create 10,000 hours for our Scottish kids very quickly? Absolutely.'

According to Hadden, however, simply building a wave pool isn't enough. For Lost Shore to work as a centre of surfing excellence, it must also be integrated into Scotland's existing surfing culture. 'The best sporting cultures have always come from places of authenticity,' he says. 'Look at All Blacks Rugby or Jamaican sprinting. The thing about cultures is, every new CEO who joins a business says "let's try and change the culture", but no – cultures are built over decades, and when you get them right, you don't have to do much work.'

To this end, Hadden has served for several years on the board of the Scottish Surfing Federation, and he also says he wants to drive customers to surf schools all around Scotland by encouraging those who have learned to surf at Lost Shore to view taking their skills to into the sea as a logical next step. 'I see [Lost Shore] as a way of creating a much much bigger surfing economy,' he says, 'so we want to stimulate the surf schools around the coast. We want to be pushing our surfers out there and saying, "Yeah, you've learned how to ride waves here, now go out to the coast and go and surf in the ocean." It's a different experience and it's an extremely fulfilling experience.'

Working in partnership with Edinburgh Napier University, Lost Shore will have a Surf Lab on site: a room adjacent to the wave pool where, among other things, surfers will be able to watch instant video replays of their waves with their coaches. And, of course, unlike in the ocean, it will be possible for surfers to ride the same wave over and over again, allowing coaches to get 'really detailed and nuanced about the exact movements they're making.' Coaching will be available for recreational surfers, too, Hadden says, both individually and in groups. 'And the better you get, the adventure only gets bigger, because you can start looking around the coast and things really open up. That's one of the things I'm most excited about seeing, people starting out on their own surfing journeys.'

'These machines make smiles' – Day One at Scotland's first wave pool

THIS was it: the moment at which surfing in Scotland officially moved from the pre-wave pool era to the post-wave pool era. Long-term effects? Too early to say. Short term effects? Lots of very happy surfers.

11 November 2024

It's 8:40am on Monday 11 November, and Ian Williams, joint chief operating officer at Edinburgh's Lost Shore surf resort, is standing proudly beside the thing he's spent the last four years helping to create: the largest inland surfing facility in Europe. In less than 20 minutes, Lost Shore's first paying customers are due to ride their first ever waves here. For now, though, the water in the pool remains completely calm. Williams? Not so much. 'I think the team are feeling a whole mixture of things,' he says. 'Excited, nervous . . . every single adjective you can think of.'

In the week prior to Lost Shore's official opening day, the internet has been awash with images of some of Scotland's top surfers giving behind-closed-doors demonstrations of what's possible on its perfect, machine-generated waves. Today, though, it's Joe Public's turn. 'At 9am this morning we'll have our first customers out surfing,' says Williams. 'The session we're going to be running is called a manoeuvres session. The manoeuvres wave sits up really well, it's quite powerful, and it enables you to turn and do manoeuvres across the face, so you need to be relatively skilled to surf it.'

The pool at Lost Shore is divided into two halves by a central spine. To the left of the spine, the waves are 'lefts', breaking from left to right as you look at them from the shore, while the waves on the other side of the spine are 'rights', breaking in the opposite direction. In general, goofy-footers – surfers who ride with their right foot forward – will tend to prefer lefts, as it's easier to see what the wave's doing ahead of you once you're up and riding; similarly, regular-footers usually prefer rights. 'More people are regular, so more people do sign up for the rights,' says Williams, who previously worked at The Wave in Bristol. 'But obviously as you progress with your surfing you look for different challenges so yeah, we'll promote that and try and get [regular-footers] going on the lefts and vice versa.'

At around 8:50am, 20 surfers head down to the water and start to paddle out towards the far end of the pool – half of them off to surf lefts, the other half looking to bag some rights. Each group has an instructor with them to explain how everything works. All of the people in the water have been surfing for years, decades in some cases, but for many this will be their first time surfing an artificial wave, so a few wave pool-specific pointers will still come in handy. At 8:55am, there's a low hum from the Wavegarden machine at the far end of the pool. On the goofy side of the spine, a glassy lump of water rears up, bounces off the sidewall and then starts peeling with almost cartoonish precision from left to right, a surfer already streaking across it; over on the right hand side of the spine, meanwhile, the same scenario is playing out, only in reverse.

Who caught the first waves of Day One? Hard to say – and that's very much on purpose. A lot of thought has gone into the design of Lost Shore to ensure that spectators are kept a reasonable distance away from the surfers. Yes, you can see enough of the surfing to be able to enjoy it, but unless you know someone's style very well, it's tricky to tell who's who. Some wave pools elsewhere in the world have been said to suffer from the 'gold-fish bowl effect', where surfers feel too much in the spotlight. However, as Lost Shore's social and health innovation lead Jamie Marshall explained in a recent interview in *The Scotsman*: 'everything about the physical design of the pool [at Lost Shore] has been informed by psychology considerations. For example: where do we want [surfers] to be able to lose themselves in the experience without people leering over them with their cellphones?'

When the first two groups of surfers emerge from the pool at the end of the 9am session, everyone is grinning from ear-to-ear, and the feedback is universally positive.

Finn Hayward, who usually surfs in North Wales, describes the wave as 'so much fun, so rippable'; according to Oscar from

Hong Kong 'the waves were firing'; Fenton Daly from San Diego calls it 'super fun, a really good time'; friends Robert and Stefan, who travelled over from Norway to surf Lost Shore, describe it as 'a very good quality wave' and 'epic' respectively. Also in the water for the 9am session: three-time Scottish national champion Mark Boyd. 'It was amazing,' he grins. 'The settings they're using for manoeuvres are really fun and really good for practising performance surfing. Half way through the session they went from the M4 fast setting, I think, to the T1, so there was a little bit of a jump [in the size of the waves] and a change in the wave shape, but both settings are really fun.'

As I'm leaving, I run into Lost Shore founder Andy Hadden, who first dreamed up the idea for the wave pool more than a decade ago. 'I was speaking to one of the guys who designed the Wavegarden technology the other day,' he says, 'and he told me "Andy, these machines don't make waves, they make smiles."' That may sound cheesy, but – based on the evidence of Lost Shore's opening day – it's also accurate.

'We had everything going against us': Next-level water photography with the Patagonia crew

IN 2024, as part of their ambitious Protect Our Ocean campaign, multinational outdoor gear brand Patagonia wanted to produce a single, inspiring image that would both convey their environmental message and reference their surfing roots. A crack team of Patagonia-sponsored surfers travelled to northern Scotland for what turned out to be a mind-bendingly complicated 3-D puzzle of a photo shoot, and took turns trying to achieve an almost impossible combination of athleticism and split-second timing for lensman Al Mackinnon to capture from beneath the waves. In the end, it was Scottish Women's Champion Phoebe Strachan and Dutch longboarder Nienke Duinmeijer who teamed up to create the perfect, unrepeatable moment.

7 December 2024

By any measure, Gabriel 'Gabe' Davies is one of the most successful surfers our North Atlantic archipelago has ever produced. Coming of age in the high-quality but also heavily polluted breaks around his native Tynemouth in the 1990s, he went on to win the British Surfing Championships four times, challenging the traditional dominance of the South West. Next, he turned his attention to big waves, bagging high-profile awards and also starring in the 2009 documentary *Waveriders*, which saw him tackling ship-killing behemoths off the coast of Ireland along with local charger Richard Fitzgerald and 11-time world champ Kelly Slater, among others. To put it mildly then, Davies is not a man to shy away from a challenge, but there were times during his most recent project when he feared he may have bitten off more than he could chew. Since 2013, when he brought his pro surfing career to a close, Davies has worked for Patagonia, the famously planet-first outdoors clothing and gear company, and he is currently their ocean marketing manager covering Europe, the Middle East and Africa.

For the last couple of years he has been working on Patagonia's Protect Our Ocean campaign, a concerted effort to persuade decision-makers all over Europe to bring an end to bottom trawling – a fishing practice that destroys vital habitats on the seabed. It's been a complex project, involving coordinating with various different environmental NGOs dotted around the continent, overseeing a series of initiatives to raise public awareness, including the production of five short documentaries, and setting up a petition calling for 'an immediate ban on bottom trawling in Marine Protected Areas and inshore zones', which has now attracted over 200,000 signatures.

Having done all this, however, Davies felt he needed a single, inspirational image to tie everything together – an image that would, as he puts it, 'connect the surf community to the environmental community, and something that might also inspire people who might never visit an NGO website to go "wow, what is this image and what are they trying to say here?"' The concept he eventually set his heart on was bold but also logistically nightmarish: an underwater shot featuring two surfers, one in the foreground holding a bellyboard with a slogan on it; the other in silhouette, streaking along a wave breaking just behind. Having enlisted the services of veteran lensman Al Mackinnon, and with some of Patagonia's top surfers at his disposal, Davies initially tried to set up a shoot for the spring of 2023, but it wasn't to be.

'We wanted the image to be relevant to the campaign,' he says, 'so it had to be somewhere where the campaign is active, so we were in Scotland, but with that come all the variables: you need sunlight, you need perfect wave conditions, you need great surfers, you can't have crowds so you need a remote location, so for all those stars to align was always going to be hard.' At the second attempt, however, at an undisclosed location somewhere in northern Scotland, everything came together and Mackinnon managed to capture the desired lightning-in-a-bottle moment: five-times Scottish surfing champion and Patagonia ambassador Phoebe Strachan rocketing across a perfectly-lit wave, with champion longboarder Nienke Duinmeijer of Holland in the foreground, holding a bellyboard bearing the slogan 'Protect the ocean so it can protect us'.

'We basically had everything going against us,' recalls Strachan. 'The time, the tide, the time of year, the daylight, all of that, so we knew we only had a very small window – pretty much just three hours – to try and get this shot. It was really difficult because the people under the water obviously couldn't see what was going on above the water and the people above the water couldn't see what was going on below, so we had to be really careful and just hope that no one was going to get run over.'

How does the Patagonia campaign apply to Scotland specifically? Perhaps the best person to answer that question is Nick Underdown of the Scottish charity and Patagonia partner organisation Open Seas, which campaigns to protect the marine environment by promoting sustainable fishing practices. 'Scotland supposedly has a network of Marine Protected Areas but many of them have no protection at all from bottom trawling,' he says. 'This is an unacceptable situation that the Scottish Government has promised coastal communities it will resolve for years, but it hasn't delivered. The Scottish Government set up Marine Protected Areas in 2014, but ten years later less than five per cent of our inshore seas are protected from fishing methods that actively scrape the seafloor. So we're left with this crazy situation where some of these areas have got OK protection in place, but many of them have no management at all, so the damage continues.'

Safe to surf? Real-time water pollution mapping for Scotland

AT THE risk of stating the obvious, if surfing is to survive and thrive in Scotland, the coastal waters where it takes place must be kept clean and safe. Since 1990, the environmental pressure group Surfers Against Sewage has campaigned tirelessly to achieve this goal, not just for the sake of surfers, but on behalf of all recreational water users. There are still far too many cases of untreated sewage being discharged into our rivers and seas, but as SAS rep Alasdair Steele points out in this interview, the recent introduction by Scottish Water of a regularly updated Overflow Map, which can alert people to potential health hazards, is at least a step in the right direction. Ideally, though, such a map wouldn't be necessary, and thanks to SAS and all the work they do holding decision-makers to account, it's possible that one fine day it might finally become redundant.

25 January 2025

Over the last couple of years, water companies in England have taken a near-constant battering in the media due to the regularity with which they have allowed untreated sewage to flow into rivers and seas. Perhaps the lowest point of many came in March last year, when it emerged that raw sewage discharges had increased by an incredible 105 per cent over the previous 12 months. Many of the maps published in print and online showing the worst-affected areas seemed to suggest that sewage was only a problem south of the Border, with all the red crosses or skull-and-crossbones icons stopping somewhere around Berwick-Upon-Tweed. Looking at these maps, Scots might have been forgiven for feeling a certain degree of relief. Unfortunately however, the situation is nowhere near as simple as 'privately owned English water companies bad, state owned Scottish Water good.' The truth is, it's still difficult to build up an accurate picture of the sewage pollution situation in Scotland as there is less data available here than in England.

Alasdair Steele, Edinburgh representative for the environmental charity Surfers Against Sewage (SAS) explains: 'There's quite a lot of spin that goes around suggesting that we don't have a problem in Scotland, but that's not true. It's just not as public as it is in England and Wales, because here less than 30 percent of the overflows are monitored.' By 'overflows', Steele is referring to CSOs or Combined Sewer Overflows, which act as a sort of systemic safety valve to reduce the risk of sewage backing up into people's homes during periods of heavy rainfall. There are just over 3,600 CSOs in Scotland, but at time of writing only around 1,000 are monitored. 'These things are dotted all around the UK,' says Steele. 'They run into rivers and they run into the sea. They were only meant to go off if you had a major storm, but obviously we've had a lot more development since our sewers were built, and that development has put more concrete onto the ground, which means there's more water flowing into them more quickly. You've also got climate change and you've got more people, so all of these things combined mean our sewage systems can't cope, so these CSOs are going off all the time.'

For all that the English sewage system is very evidently falling apart in places, it is at least now possible for water users south of the Border to determine whether the water near them is safe to swim in or not. Since 2014, real-time data from CSOs around the country has been fed into an app developed by SAS called The Safer Seas & Rivers Service, which enables people to see at a glance whether there has been recent discharge from a CSO. Steele is keen to stress that things are now moving in the right direction in Scotland: on 16 December 2024, Scottish Water launched an interactive Overflow Map, billed as 'a near real-time map show[ing] the status of monitored overflows and the duration of any overflow events to help better inform our customers.'

However, he also points out that, with only around 30 per cent of CSOs included so far, the picture is nowhere near complete. 'It's great that this is coming,' he says, 'but we need to move fast, so we need to get all our CSOs monitored, and we also need this to link in to the Safer Seas & Rivers Service app, because it's already got a quarter of a million users – it's a much easier way for people to find the information.'

Clearly informing people about likely risks of sewage pollution is vitally important, but it's only a short-term fix – the long-term goal of SAS and other groups working alongside them is to prevent pollution events from happening in the first place. Fixing antiquated sewage systems will take both time and money, however, and from the perspective of an environmental pressure group, this is a more problematic thing to push for in Scotland than it is in England. South of the Border, it's easy to attack well-paid CEOs of private water companies for letting an outdated sewage system rot while raking in profits, and the general public are more likely to be sympathetic to calls for – say – shareholder dividends being cut in order to help fund infrastructure upgrades. In Scotland, however, Scottish Water is a public body, so any upgrades will require increased public expenditure: an altogether tougher sell. Still, Steele is optimistic. 'We can't just suddenly sort these things out,' he says. 'What we can do, though, in the short term, is we can tell people if there's an issue. We're not going to turn round and say, "we need to put hundreds of millions of pounds into the sewage system straight away", so in the meantime, let's make sure that if you want to go swimming or kayaking or surfing, in the sea or in a river, you at least know whether it's polluted.'

Epilogue

Ben Larg takes Scottish surfing to bold new heights at Nazaré

JUST before 4pm on 17 February, my phone pinged with a WhatsApp message from Marti Larg. 'Ben just got an entry to WSL big wave comp tomorrow' it said, followed by a 'wide eyes' emoji. I checked the World Surf League website and sure enough, there was Ben's name on the list of participating athletes for the following day's Nazaré Big Wave Challenge in Portugal. A moment later, another message landed: 'Garrett Mcnamara gave Ben his spot.' It's one thing get a chance to take part in one of the most prestigious big wave surfing competitions on the planet, but to be granted a place by one of the true legends of the sport? Fairytale stuff. With waves forecast to be in the 25–40-foot range, if Ben had simply turned up, made it to safety on a couple of medium-sized ones and finished flat last, it would still have been an incredible achievement. He wasn't just there to make up the numbers though – this was his big opportunity to show the world what he could do, and he wasn't about to waste it. As I watched him rack up one solid score after another on the live stream while the commentators waxed lyrical about his fearless approach, I thought back to the pint-sized kid I'd seen Marti pushing into waves on a longboard at Balephuil all those years ago; to Chris Noble's insistence, back in 2010, that Scotland could produce a pro surfer one day; to Andy Bennetts and Scotland's surfing pioneers of the 1960s and 70s, trying to figure out where the best waves were by trial and error; and to Neva MacDonald-Haig, sliding around in the shorebreak at Machrihanish on her modified coffin lid. All the many different strands of Scotland's surfing story seemed to coalesce, just for a few moments, as a 20 year-old from Tiree painted bold, beautiful, curving lines across some of the most majestic canvases in all the surfing world.

1 March 2025

On 17 February, 20-year-old Scottish surfer Ben Larg received a life-changing phone call. On the other end of the line was Hawaiian big wave legend Garrett McNamara, star of the HBO documentary *100 Foot Wave*. McNamara had decided not to compete in the Nazaré Big Wave Challenge in Portugal the following day – an invitation-only event that pits the best big wave riders in the world against each other in super-sized surf. Would Ben like to take his place?

Designed to showcase tow-in surfing, in which surfers are slingshotted into waves on ropes attached to the back of jet skis, the Nazaré contest brings together a select group of big wave specialists and divides them into pairs, with the members of each team taking it in turns to surf and drive the ski. In order to ensure optimal conditions, this year's event had a five-month waiting period, running from 1 November 2024 to 31 March 2025. When Larg took McNamara's call, the surf forecasting service Surfline was predicting 25-40ft surf for the following day. Serious conditions. Larg didn't hesitate.

'I think maybe Garrett decided it was time to pass the baton,' he says of their conversation. 'He was like, "Yeah, you go for it, kid."'

Given the last-minute nature of Larg's entry into the event and his lack of competitive experience (this was to be his first ever appearance in a big wave contest) it would have been easy to write him off as a makeweight – a little-known big wave charger who might perhaps snag a passable wave or two and raise a few curious eyebrows with his unusual country of origin. However, if the Tiree native was a relative unknown on the evening of 17 February, by the evening of the 18th he was well and truly on the surfing world's radar. Not only did he and his tow-in partner Andrew Cotton of Devon finish third in the team competition, Larg also placed third in the men's individual standings, ahead of some of the most famous names in the sport, including Kai Lenny of Hawaii and Nic von Rupp of Portugal.

One of the commentators on the live stream of the event on Red Bull TV was Carlos Burle of Brazil – a true giant of the big wave surfing world, now retired. At one point, watching Larg convert almost all of his forward momentum into a full-blooded mid-face hack, at a moment when even seasoned big wave riders might have opted for something a little more conservative, he exclaimed: 'Beautiful! He's approaching a thirty-foot wave like it's a two-foot wave!'

That just about summed up Larg's no-guts-no-glory attitude. The teams each had two 40-minute heats in which to impress the judges, with their best two scores counting towards an overall total, and Larg surfed every wave he caught as if it might have been his last.

To those who have been following Larg's career closely, his remarkable Nazaré result might not seem quite so remarkable. This, after all, is the lad who rode a 30-foot monster at Mullaghmore in Ireland at the age of just 14, was tackling even bigger waves at Nazaré aged 16 and picked up a Red Bull sponsorship deal thanks to his big wave exploits at the age of 17. He and Cotton had been training together in Nazaré for much of the winter by the time McNamara's phone call came in, so if there was ever going to be a moment for him to show the world what he could do, this was undoubtedly it. Still, Larg is taking nothing for granted – when I speak to him on the phone a couple of hours after the Nazaré contest he says he's 'super-delighted' and very modestly describes his third place finish as 'a good result'.

Unlike most of the competitors in the event, who aimed to ride lefts (waves breaking from surfer's right to left) towards the beach of Praia do Norte, Larg and Cotton decided to focus on the rights breaking towards the cliffs beneath Nazaré's iconic lighthouse. It was a high-risk strategy, requiring a couple of heart-in-mouth jet ski rescues, but one that paid off.

'Obviously, the right goes into the rocks, so it's a bit dodgy,' Larg explains, understating the case somewhat. 'But the rescues were good and we never lost boards or anything.' A surfboard, if hurled against those cliffs by a 30-foor wall of whitewater, wouldn't be so much lost as pulped.

For all that Larg and Cotton were mostly concentrating on going right, Larg's highest score actually came from a left. On perhaps the largest wave he'd caught all day, he initially made as if to head towards the cliffs but then swung around and went rocketing off in the opposite direction. A long, committed bottom turn just ahead of an avalanche of whitewater projected him high up onto the wave's face, at which point a weight shift from his heels to his toes allowed him to draw a beautiful, arcing carve. Another high-speed turn off the bottom of the wave sent him soaring up towards its crest once more, but this time, with the lip beginning to pitch in front of him, he took the only exit route available, launching himself high into the air and landing well clear of the ensuing explosion. As Chris Coté, another of the commentators on the live stream, said of Larg: 'He's already proven himself, but he's still got a lot more to give.' Who can say where he'll go from here?

Acknowledgements

Thank you to all the people who have shared their surfing stories with me over the last couple of decades, but in particular to serial contributors Andy Bennetts, Will Beeslaar, Mark Boyd, Mark Cameron, Sam Christopherson, Andy Hadden, Ben Larg, Derek MacLeod, Chris Noble, William Watson, Paul Stark, Alasdair Steele, Phoebe Strachan and Craig Sutherland. Thaks also to all those who have provided images for this book, particularly Malcolm Anderson, Janeanne Gilchrist and Mike Guest.

Thanks to my extended surfing family: Steve 'Surfer Steve' Cox (no relation), Phil Hamilton, Ed, Tarini, Rosa and Mae Mellanby-Chetty, and Pete, Kim, Stanley and Molly Grant. Thanks to Marti and Iona Larg for many warm welcomes to Tiree over the years, and to Ben Larg for providing this book with its fairytale ending.

Thanks to Alison Gray and Will Slater on the *Scotsman Magazine* for making my words make sense to non-surfers, to Kerry Black for her help with the *Scotsman* archives, to Paul Smith and Andrew Simmons at Birlinn for their patience and flexibility with deadlines, and to Jan Rutherford and David Robinson for their encouragement with this project.

Thanks to Sharon and Sam Cox, to my brother Simon for being my first and longest-suffering surf buddy, and to our parents, Gill and Stephen, for making sure we spent a big part of our childhood in and around the sea. Finally, thank you to Joanna, Matthew and Ben, for all our adventures so far, and for those still to come.